MW00697876

IN LIVING COLOR
The Curriculum of Creation

In Living Color

Author: Stephen Davey
Illustrations: Adam Dohrmann
Editor: Jarl K. Waggoner
Body Layout: Kristin Preston
Photo of Stephen: Brian W. Downs
ISBN: 978-1-944189-43-3

Unless otherwise noted, all Scripture quotations are from the New American Standard Bible® (NASB), © 1960, 1962, 1963, 1968, 1971, 1972, 1973, 1975, 1977, 1995 by the Lockman Foundation. Used by permission. www.Lockman.org

Scripture quotations marked MSG are from The Message. Copyright © by Eugene H. Peterson 1993, 1994, 1995, 1996, 2000, 2001, 2002. Used by permission of Tyndale House Publishers, Inc.

Scripture quotations marked KJV are from the King James Version of the Bible.

Scripture quotations marked ESV are from The Holy Bible, English Standard Version® (ESV®), copyright ©2001 by Crossway, a publishing ministry of Good News Publishers. Used by permission. All rights reserved.

Published by Charity House Publishers

Charity House Publishers, Inc.
2703 Jones Franklin Road
Suite 105
Cary, NC 27518
USA

With heartfelt gratitude to my friend and colleague
~ Ken Ham ~
For his faithful courage and visionary creativity
In giving the world a biblical understanding
Of the creative handiwork of God.

CONTENTS

THE CURRICULUM OF CREATION

Leonardo di ser Piero da Vinci (1452–1519) was an Italian humanist of the Renaissance period. He immersed himself in science, mathematics, engineering, invention, anatomy, sculpting, architecture, botany, music, writing, cartography, literature, and other studies. With all his diverse knowledge of several disciplines, however, he became most famous for his world-renowned paintings *The Last Supper* and *Mona Lisa*.[1]

Leonardo once wrote that "an average human looks without *seeing*, listens without *hearing*, touches without *feeling*, eats without *tasting*, inhales without *awareness* of odor or fragrance, and talks without *thinking*." He called the five senses "the ministers of the soul"[2] and spent his life developing creative observation.

He never went anywhere without his notebooks, in which he recorded ideas and observations. His journals contain his most ingenious ideas—a helicopter-like contraption he called an ornithopter, an underwater diving suit, and a robotic soldier. Seven thousand pages of his journals have been preserved since his death in 1519. A few years ago, Bill Gates purchased a seventy-two-page notebook of Leonardo's for $30 million.[3]

Leonardo's words challenge the average human being not just to look but to see, not just to listen but to hear, not just to eat but to taste, and not just to breathe but to take in the fragrance. How much more should we Christians train ourselves and our senses to ultimately give praise and glory to our creator God.

In his commentary on Psalm 19, James Montgomery Boice wrote perceptively that God has revealed Himself in two Books: a Big Book and a Little Book.[4]

The Big Book is the universe—all of creation that surrounds us. Theologians call this *general revelation* because it is available and discernible to the senses of everyone. Through general revelation we get the opportunity not merely to look but to *see* God's creation and marvel at our amazing Creator.

The Little Book is the Bible. Theologians refer to it as *special revelation*. It is the revealed word from God that fills in all the blanks. Creation reveals *what* God did; the Bible reveals *why* God did it. Creation displays His power; the Bible describes His purpose.

Frankly, it's high time for Christians to take their Bibles *and* binoculars and go for a hike. It's time to do more than just look around; it's time to see, to sit out on the back deck and not just stare into space but take note of something specific God has created. It's time to travel, even if by way of a book, and to begin exploring something in God's creation.

Phillip Keller, the author of a wonderful book entitled *A Shepherd Looks at Psalm 23*, also wrote a lesser-known book entitled *Still Waters*. This book is a collection of personal observations about nature, animals, and creation. Keller says that God is the divine Composer, and we should start listening to His music with whatever senses we have at our disposal by seeing, hearing, touching, smelling, and tasting.[5]

God's creative handiwork is displayed before us in *living color*, and there are at least ten reasons why every believer should take the time to truly see, touch, and taste His amazing creation.

CREATION IS THE UNDENIABLE
ANNOUNCEMENT OF THE REALITY OF GOD

> The heavens are telling of the glory of God; and their expanse is declaring the work of His hands. Day to day pours forth speech, and night to night reveals knowledge. (Psalm 19:1-2)

One paraphrase reads: "God's glory is on tour in the skies, God-craft on exhibit across the horizon. Madame Day holds classes every morning, Professor Night lectures every evening" (MSG).

When you look around, what do you see? Job described the moon, the clouds, and the earth, which hangs upon nothing, as simply the *fringes* of God's ways (Job 26:7-14). The Puritans used to say that God left large footprints throughout the universe.

In Psalm 19:4, the author David declared, "Their line has gone out through all the earth, and their utterances to the end of the world." The Hebrew word translated "line" can be translated "voice" or "cry."[6] Although verse 3 says that no speech or words come from the heavens, they still have a voice that reveals God's glory.

Several years ago, the European Space Agency (ESA) and the National Aeronautics and Space Administration (NASA) began to record radio waves emitted by the Sun, Saturn, Jupiter, Mars, moons, comets, and Earth's atmosphere. While probes carrying microphones record direct sounds, others rely on technology to convert electromagnetic vibrations into audio signals.[7] Now that scientists have a better grasp of gravitational waves, they can *hear* the universe.[8] NASA has even cataloged individual sounds from space.[9]

Imagine that. We are surrounded by the music of creation. The universe truly does sing. The heavens *audibly* broadcast the glory of God, and we have just begun to hear it. Perhaps one day the Lord will allow us to hear in its fullness the music of the universe as it declares God's glory.

Like the famous painter Picasso, who dipped his thumb in the paint and then rolled it on the canvas as his signature, God's signature has been rolled all over the portrait of creation.

THE STUDY OF CREATION PROVIDES A CURRICULUM FOR WISE LIVING

Go to the ant, O sluggard, observe her ways and be wise, which, having no chief, officer or ruler, prepares her food in the summer and gathers her provision in the harvest. (Proverbs 6:6-8)

Solomon teaches here that studying the organization, determination, and work ethic of ants can make one wiser in life. This is not just good counsel for the lazy but a reminder that there are important lessons to be learned from creation.

The psalmist wrote, "Great are the works of the Lord; they are studied by all who delight in them" (Psalm 111:2). The Hebrew verb translated "studied" (*darash*) means to research, to make careful, diligent study. The works to which the psalmist refers include both the work of creation and the work of redemption.[10] Such works are studied "by all who delight in them."

Since the psalmist adds in verse 4 that God "has made His wonders to be remembered," we should find ways to remember them. Maybe that means painting a picture of something in nature, taking a photograph of an animal, a flower, or sunset, or keeping a journal of what we observe when we hike through the woods.

The great English preacher of the nineteenth century, Charles H. Spurgeon, wrote of Psalm 111:

God's works are worthy of our researches, they yield us instruction and pleasure wonderfully blended. . . . The hidden wisdom of God is the most marvelous part of his works, and hence those who do not look below the surface miss the best part of what he would teach us.[11]

The psalmist encourages us not just to passively look but to actively see, think, and connect what we *see* to what God has *said*.

If you ever wondered whether God would approve of your visit to the beach or fishing on a boat, the psalmist writes:

> Those who go down to the sea in ships, who do business on great waters; they have seen the works of the LORD, and His wonders in the deep. . . . Who is wise? Let him give heed to these things, and consider the lovingkindnesses of the LORD. (Psalm 107:23-24, 43)

In other words, go ahead! Sail, fish, and take that hike in the mountains. And then leave each adventure saying, "God is faithful! He is dependable in every detail."

THE IMMENSITY OF THE UNIVERSE EXPOSES THE CHASM BETWEEN GOD'S MIND AND OURS

Isaiah was deeply moved by this truth as he wrote:

> Who [but God] has measured the waters in the hollow of His hand, and marked off the heavens by the span, and calculated the dust of the earth by the measure, and weighed the mountains in a balance and the hills in a pair of scales? Who has directed the Spirit of the LORD, or as His counselor has informed Him? (Isaiah 40:12-13)

Isaac Newton said it well: "What we know is a drop, what we do not know is a vast ocean. The admirable arrangement and harmony of the universe could only have come from the plan of an omniscient and omnipotent being."[12]

The more we study creation, the greater God becomes in our eyes.

CREATION CONFIRMS THE SURPASSING VALUE OF HUMAN BEINGS TO ALL OTHER CREATURES

Human beings are worth more than animals, trees, rocks, or rivers. Your value isn't inferior or equal to animals; it's *greater*.

The Bible never refers to the human being as a more sophisticated animal. Unfortunately, years of evolutionary propaganda have drilled that lie into us. And so today many people believe humans have no more right to Planet Earth than a pine tree.

At the dawn of creation history, the triune God announced:

> "Let Us make man in Our image, according to Our likeness; and let them rule over the fish of the sea and over the birds of the sky and over the cattle and over all the earth, and over every creeping thing that creeps on the earth." (Genesis 1:26)

Since we alone possess the image of God, we have been endowed with certain attributes and privileges animals are not given. For example, we have an eternal spirit that will never pass away; a conscience and a moral compass so that we can choose right instead of wrong; and the ability to communicate with, worship, and honor the creator God. We are also the objects of the redemptive plan of God fulfilled through the death of God's own Son—Jesus Christ.

Our world objects, saying, "Who are we to say we are more important than the birds and the trees? Who are we to say we have more value?"

Well, Jesus actually said that in His most famous sermon:

> "Look at the birds of the air, they do not sow, nor reap nor gather into barns, and yet your heavenly Father feeds them. *Are you not worth much more* than they?" (Matthew 6:26)

This perspective explains why God considers murdering another human being a violation of His moral law (Genesis 9:6; Exodus

20:13). However, killing animals and eating them is neither murder nor a violation of God's moral law (Acts 10:9-16).

Even those who deny the supremacy of human life acknowledge it when they shudder at the thought of someone killing and eating his neighbor! They'll be happy to lock that cannibal up for a very long time. Eating a hamburger is an entirely different matter! In fact, it's part of God's created order. God instructed Noah after the Flood, saying:

> "Every moving thing that is alive shall be food for you; I give all to you, as I gave the green plant." (Genesis 9:3)

God approves a barbecue just as much as He does a salad . . . I praise God for *that*!

STUDYING THE UNIVERSE MAKES US APPRECIATE GOD'S ATTENTION TO US

> When I consider Your heavens, the work of Your fingers, the moon and the stars, which You have ordained; what is man that You take thought of him, and the son of man that You care for him? (Psalm 8:3-4)

Famous people usually have no time for "unimportant" people, except for handing out autographs.

In Psalm 8, David expressed his amazement at why God, having created something as vast as the universe, cares about little, insignificant *us*.

Contrast this with the despair created by evolution. The evolutionist looks at the immensity of the universe and becomes utterly lost in his insignificance.

Before he died, Carl Sagan, the popular television host and evolutionist, wrote with that same despair:

> Our planet is a lonely speck in the great enveloping cosmic dark. In our obscurity, in all this vastness, there is no hint that help will come from elsewhere to save us from ourselves.[13]

How vastly different this is from God's created plan. He designed us to glorify Him now and then throughout eternity as His redeemed, glorified, immortalized host of heaven! The best is yet to come . . . there is no despair in that!

ANIMALS PROVIDE A DIVINE ANSWER FOR CRIPPLING ANXIETY

"For this reason I say to you, do not be worried about your life, as to what you will eat or what you will drink; nor for your body, as to what you will put on. Is not life more than food, and the body more than clothing? Look at the birds of the air, that they do not sow, nor reap nor gather into barns, and yet your heavenly Father feeds them. Are you not worth much more than they? And who of you by being worried can add a single hour to his life?" (Matthew 6:25-27)

Jesus wasn't saying here that the birds just lie around and wait for God the Father to feed them. He meant that God has created within them the instinctive capacity to find whatever is necessary to live. He created them that way because He cares about them. And if He *cares* about the birds, how much more will He care about *us*, who are so much more valuable.

No animal was ever created in the image of God, so no animal will be a joint heir with Christ in the coming kingdom. But you and I and all who have placed their faith in Christ Jesus will!

And between here and there, God has promised to care for us, including all our material and earthly needs. Such care is far above and beyond His care for other creatures of the earth precisely because of the eternal value with which we are endowed by the Creator Himself.

EXPLORING THE NATURAL WORLD PROVIDES HEALING FOR A BROKEN SPIRIT

The enemy has persecuted my soul; he has crushed my life to the ground; he has made me dwell in dark places, like those who have long been dead. Therefore my spirit is overwhelmed within me; my heart is appalled within me. I remember the days of old; I meditate on all Your doings; I muse on the work of Your hands. (Psalm 143:3-5)

The Hebrew verb translated "meditate" in verse 5 is the same word used in Joshua 1:8, where the Lord commanded Joshua to meditate on God's Word day and night. "Muse" stands parallel to "meditate" and is essentially synonymous in meaning. David is telling his readers that contemplating, meditating on, the creative and redemptive works of God is what restores the spirit of the one who is persecuted, beaten down, and discouraged.

Now, don't misunderstand the psalmist here. He isn't equating nature with Scripture in terms of its value. However, he makes it clear that the handiwork of God has incredible value to the human spirit and shouldn't be ignored.

Job demanded answers from God regarding the incredible suffering he endured. When God finally spoke to Job, it's interesting that instead of giving Job answers, God took him on a tour of creation.

When the tour was over, Job essentially responded to God, "I have seen your creative splendor, majesty, wisdom, and power, and that's enough of an answer for me" (see Job 38–42).

THE ORDER OF THE UNIVERSE PROVIDES AN ANTIDOTE FOR INSECURITY

In his book *The Grave Robber*, Mark Batterson reproduced an interesting article entitled "A Stellar 360." It reads:

It might *seem* like you're sitting still right now (hopefully you're not reading and walking), but it's an illusion of miraculous proportions. The pale blue dot you're sitting on is spinning around its axis at a speed of roughly 1,000 miles per hour. Every 24 hours, planet Earth pulls off a *literal* stellar 360. We're also hurtling through space at an average velocity of 67,108 miles per hour.

That's . . . a lot faster than a bullet. Better yet, it's 87 times faster than the speed of sound. Feeling like you didn't get much done today? Well, you did travel 1,599,793 miles through space. Best of all, the Milky Way is spinning like a galactic pinwheel at the dizzying rate of 483,000 mph. If that isn't miraculous, I don't know what is. Then again, when was the last time I thanked the God of heavens for keeping us in orbit? Not recently! "Lord, I wasn't sure we'd make the full rotation today, but You did it again! Whew… Crisis averted." We just don't pray that way.[14]

What an interesting antidote to anxiety: If you can trust God, without even thinking about it, to keep the galaxy spinning according to His will—if you can trust God for something that big—you can certainly trust Him for something as small as keeping your own life on course according to His plan and His design.

The songwriter put it this way:

> *This is my Father's world,*
> *And to my listening ears*
> *All nature sings, and round me rings*
> *The music of the spheres.*
> *This is my Father's world:*
> *I rest me in the thought*
> *Of rocks and trees, of skies and seas—*
> *His hand the wonders wrought.*[15]

CREATION WILL SERVE AS THE EVIDENCE IN THE COURTROOM OF GOD'S ETERNAL JUDGMENT OF UNBELIEVERS

For the wrath of God is revealed from heaven against all ungodliness and unrighteousness of men who suppress the truth in unrighteousness, because that which is known about God is evident within them; for God made it evident to them. For since the creation of the world His invisible attributes, His eternal power and divine nature, have been clearly seen, being understood through what has been made, so that they are without excuse. For even though they knew God, they did not honor Him as God or give thanks, but they became futile in their speculations, and their foolish heart was darkened. Professing to be wise, they became fools. (Romans 1:18-22)

When all unbelievers in human history stand before God to be judged at the great white throne, thus ending human history as we know it, they will be without excuse. And they will be without excuse, not because they heard the gospel of *Christ* and rejected it or because they heard the gospel of *conscience* and denied it. Rather, they will be without excuse because they heard, saw, tasted, smelled, and felt the gospel of *creation* and suppressed the evident truth creation reveals about the Creator, forged speculations that denied the truth, and refused to honor the Creator.

Creation will serve as the final evidence of the unbeliever's ungrateful heart that chose to suppress the obvious truth of a Creator. And an eternal verdict of guilt and judgment will be delivered.

For those who have not yet trusted in Christ as creator God and eternal Savior, there is still time even today. Our Lord and Savior patiently waits, desiring that all would repent and call upon Him in faith.

CREATION LEADS US TO CONTINUAL AMAZEMENT AND JOYFUL PRAISE OF OUR CREATOR GOD

By the word of the Lord the heavens were made, and by the breath of His mouth all their host. He gathers the waters of the sea together as a heap; He lays up the deeps in storehouses. Let all the earth fear the Lord; let all the inhabitants of the world stand in awe of Him. For He spoke, and it was done; He commanded, and it stood fast. (Psalm 33:6-9)

In this psalm, we are compelled to fear the Creator and stand in awe of Him *because* of His creative power. Awe can be defined as "an emotion variously combining dread, veneration, and wonder that is inspired by the sacred or sublime."[16] God has designed us to worship Him in awe as we observe and consider His amazing creation.

Neuroscientists have detected the astounding effects of *awe* in the brain. At a recent meeting of the Organization for Human Brain Mapping, researchers revealed that "feelings of awe shut down the brain's default mode network, an area thought to relate to our sense of self. This would explain why we feel like we lose a sense of *ourselves* in moments of awe. We become less aware of ourselves and more connected with those around us."[17]

It's true, isn't it? When we stand before an incredibly beautiful sunset or at the base of a waterfall, we forget about ourselves. We are swept up in the awareness of something or *Someone* far greater than ourselves.

The scientific community is simply catching up to ancient truths revealed by God's Spirit. The psalmist wrote: "They who dwell in the ends of the earth stand in awe of Your signs; You make the dawn and the sunset shout for joy" (Psalm 65:8).

When we stand in awe of God's wonders, we lose our focus on self and get lost in a sense of God's greatness, majesty, and creative glory. This leads us to thank and worship the Lord for His amazing creation.

Skeptics attempt to explain in various ways the awe they feel at times. But for us who know the Lord of creation, His creation surrounding us and in us produces *pure* worship. Isaac Watts expressed this truth well when he wrote:

> *I sing the mighty power of God*
> *That made the mountains rise,*
> *That spread the flowing seas abroad,*
> *And built the lofty skies.*

I sing the wisdom that ordained
The sun to rule the day;
The moon shines full at His command
And all the stars obey.

I sing the goodness of the Lord
That filled the earth with food;
He formed the creatures with His Word
And then pronounced them good.
Lord, how Thy wonders are displayed
Where'er I turn my eye:
If I survey the ground I tread
Or gaze upon the sky!

There's not a plant or flower below
But makes Thy glories known;
And clouds arise and tempests blow
By order from Thy throne;
While all that borrows life from Thee
Is ever in Thy care,
And ev'rywhere that man can be,
Thou God art present there.[18]

CHAPTER ONE

A VOLCANO AND THE AGE OF EARTH

One of the major, ongoing philosophical disputes in the world relates to the origin of the universe and of life. All hypotheses regarding origins fall into one of two categories: *naturalism* or *supernaturalism*. Naturalism argues that the origin of everything can be explained scientifically without any need of supernatural interference or even existence. Supernaturalism teaches that everything was supernaturally created by one being who is superior to all material and immaterial elements.

Naturalists propose that a massive explosion created the extremely complex and organized universe, an event known as the big bang. Following the theory of evolution, astronomers then estimate that the universe is some 14 billion years old. Earth is said to be 4.5 billion years old.[1]

On the opposite side of the spectrum, Scripture teaches creationism—that the universe and life therein were supernaturally created by God; He spoke, and it was so (Genesis 1). If we take the biblical record of creation and subsequent genealogies at face value, then the Lord created all there is in only six days (Genesis 2:1-3; Exodus 20:11), and the earth is around six thousand years old.

In light of this conclusion, skeptics raise one main question: If the earth is so young, why does it appear so much older?

The earth appears to be old *only* if one holds to the evolutionary model of *uniformitarianism*, which assumes that "processes that alter the Earth are uniform through time."[2] This means that whatever is happening in nature around us has been happening that way since the beginning of earth's *evolutionary* birthdate—4.5 billion years ago.

Therefore, assuming the *normal* rate of erosion we can measure today, the Grand Canyon would have to be some six *million* years old.[3]

But what if something out of the ordinary took place?

LOOKING OLD

Genesis 7 records that an extremely unusual event took place, something that had never happened before:

> In the six hundredth year of Noah's life, in the second month, on the seventeenth day of the month, on the same day all the fountains of the great deep burst open, and the floodgates of the sky were opened. The rain fell upon the earth for forty days and forty nights. On the very same day Noah and Shem and Ham and Japheth, the sons of Noah, and Noah's wife and the three wives of his sons with them, entered the ark, they and every beast after its kind, and all the cattle after their kind, and every creeping thing that creeps on the earth after its kind, and every bird after its kind, all sorts of birds. So they went into the ark to Noah, by twos of all flesh in which was the breath of life. Those that entered, male and female of all flesh, entered as God had commanded him; and the LORD closed it behind him. Then the flood came upon the earth for forty days, and the water increased and lifted up the ark, so that it rose above the earth. The water prevailed and increased greatly upon the earth, and the ark floated on the surface of the water. The water prevailed more and more upon the earth, so that all the high mountains everywhere under the heavens were covered. The water prevailed fifteen cubits higher, and the mountains were covered. All flesh that moved on the earth perished, birds and cattle and beasts and every swarming thing that swarms upon the earth, and all mankind; of all that was on the dry land, all in whose

nostrils was the breath of the spirit of life, died . . . the water prevailed upon the earth one hundred and fifty days. (Genesis 7:11-24)

The Bible describes this great flood as a unique event that engulfed the planet, rapidly changing the features of the planet. But was the flood of Noah's day really global, or was it actually a regional flood, as many even within the church insist?

Consider the following evidence for a global flood:

- The biblical language clearly indicates the flood was global (note the repetition of the word *all*).

- The apostle Peter used the events of a global flood as an illustration of a future global firestorm of God's wrath (2 Peter 3:5-10), and Jesus Christ Himself used the flood as a reference to His global judgment yet to come when He returns to earth (Matthew 24:37-39).

- God promised that He would never again "destroy the earth" with a flood (see the rainbow as the sign of the covenant promise in Genesis 9:8-17). If the flood of Noah was regional, then God has repeatedly broken His promise to people all around the world, for rainfall annually causes local flooding throughout the world.

- If the flood was local, animals and people simply could have migrated to another region for safety.

- If the flooding was local, Noah also could have migrated, saving more than a hundred years of his life building an enormous boat.

- Finally, the widespread fossil record, with fossils found in many puzzling locations, indicates the flood was global.

Not only did rain pour down from above, but channels of water beneath the surface of the ground and the ocean floor also burst forth. This action also would have released steam and lava in volcanic eruptions.

It's difficult to imagine the tumbling of the earth's surface that resulted from massive flooding, erosion, and the tsunamis that resulted from underwater plate shifting. This massive commotion sent great walls of water racing across the continents.

As the continents uplifted and shifted, mountain chains buckled up. Entire mountain ranges previously nonexistent appeared as they were forced upward. The global flood thus accomplished in a year's time what erosion and natural processes (uniformitarianism) could not create in millions of years.

It's interesting to note that the mountains of Ararat, where the ark finally came to rest, are made of molten lava, like many of the mountain ranges in the Pacific Northwest. These are called volcanic mountains because they are the result of multiple eruptions. The very mountains Noah's ark came to rest upon had been pushed upward during the flood event by molten lava from deep inside the earth's crust.

The flood also accounts for the presence of marine fossils on the tops of such high volcanic mountain ranges. Fossils of ocean creatures are found even on the peak of Mount Everest 29,000 feet above sea level.[4]

In light of discoveries like these, the naturalistic scientific community is acknowledging the possibility of some sort of catastrophe that shaped the topography of the earth and caused millions of animal fossils and sediment to be laid down on a global scale.[5]

Geology is starting to catch up with Genesis.

When our twin sons were in second grade, a scientist came to their school with dinosaur fossils to give a special presentation. I decided to go to the school that day to listen in on the presentation. I wanted to know what to talk about and how to explain those things to my sons from a creationist, biblical worldview.

I stood at the back of the auditorium in an alcove under a little balcony. My boys had no idea I was there. At the end of the presentation, the specialist said, "You know, we're not sure what caused so many dinosaurs to be killed around the same time, after which they pretty much went extinct. We don't really know what happened." At that moment, Seth raised his hand. I wondered what in the world he was raising his hand for since the speaker wasn't asking for questions!

The scientist spotted him and said, "Yes?"

Seth hollered out, "It was the flood!"

The lecturer responded, "Well, that is *possible*."

Indeed, the flood refashioned the earth, as mountains were pushed upward and ocean valleys, river basins, and canyons were carved out, suddenly making the earth *look* more beautiful—and much older than it really was.

OLD! OLD? NEW!

A favorite argument evolutionists use for an old earth is the creation of coal. Naturalists explain the formation of coal as follows:

> The conditions that would eventually create coal began to develop about 300 million years ago, during the Carboniferous period. During this time, the Earth was covered in wide, shallow seas and dense forests. The seas occasionally flooded the forested areas, trapping plants and algae at the bottom of a swampy wetland. Over time, the plants (mostly mosses) and algae were buried and compressed under the weight of overlying mud and vegetation.
>
> As the plant debris sifted deeper under the Earth's surface, it encountered increased temperatures and higher pressure. Mud and acidic water prevented the plant matter from coming into contact with oxygen. Due to this, the plant matter decomposed at a very slow rate and retained most of its carbon (source of energy).
>
> These areas of buried plant matter are called peat bogs. Peat bogs store massive amounts of carbon many meters underground. . . . Under the right conditions, peat transforms into coal through a process called carboniza-

tion. Carbonization takes place under incredible heat and pressure.[6]

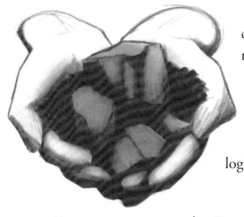

300 million years to form? Hardly!

If the conditions that formed coal did, in fact, begin about 300 million years ago, then the planet evidently is quite old.

It seems that God has answered yet again in our own generation through one of the greatest geological events; an event considered by many to be the most catastrophic event in the history of the United States.[7] The volcanic eruption of Mount St. Helens in Washington state in 1980 became a laboratory to study the results of a massive eruption and local flooding. The results have been staggering.

On May 18, 1980, the beautiful setting of Mount St. Helens was dramatically changed. The top and side of the mountain blew off in a massive explosion equaling the detonation of several nuclear bombs. The topography of a wide area surrounding the mountain was instantly changed. If naturalist scientists unaware of the eruption had stumbled onto the scenery a decade later, they could easily imagine that it took millions of years to carve out the canyons, gullies, and lakes around Mount St. Helens.

Mt. St. Helens

Leveled trees could have built 600,000 homes

Erupted May 18th, 1980

26

The volcanic blast from Mount St. Helens traveled at 650 miles per hour and destroyed the forests in the surrounding 230 square miles. The blast leveled 3.2 billion feet of timber in less than ten minutes. Douglas fir trees 200 feet tall were snapped like toothpicks.[8]

As the side of the mountain slid into nearby Spirit Lake, it sent a wave of water up into the neighboring forest areas. As the water returned to the lake, it carried four million trees with it, creating a massive log mat.[9]

One of the most shocking by-products was discovered only five years later, in 1985. Bark that had shed from the enormous floating log mat on Spirit Lake had intermingled with volcanic sediment and sunk to the bottom of the lake, forming a layer of peat more than three feet thick. "The Spirit Lake peat is texturally and composition-ally similar to the coarse content of coal beds, which secular geologists believe require many thousands of years to accumulate."[10] Right there in Spirit Lake—in living color—scientists witnessed the first forma-tion stage of coal beds in only five years, not thousands of years. "The lesson from Spirit Lake is that coal beds can and do form rapidly, due to catastrophic destruction of forests, not the slow and gradual growth of plants in swamps."[11]

The standard geological, uniformitarian viewpoint is that it takes one thousand years to form *one inch* of coal. But in Spirit Lake scien-tists found, not one inch, but *three feet* of coal in its early formation!

Imagine what a global flood, along with massive volcanic erup-tions, would do to earth's vegetation. All the forests immediately tumbled together with lava, sediment, and water, and the timber underwent a high degree of heat and pressure. The coal beds that exist today were most certainly formed a few thousand years ago in the global flood.

The observable scientific evidence at Spirit Lake with regard to coal formation is consistent with a young earth.

But that's not all. In June of 1992, scientists took samples of vol-canic rock from the site at Mount St. Helens and dated them using the standard potassium-argon method. Although the rocks had been created by the eruption just a few years earlier, this dating method concluded the rocks were 350,000 years old, and the minerals packed inside the rocks in the eruption were dated at *2.4 million years old.*[12]

Geologists were stunned. The traditional radioactive dating methods used to date the planet were shown to be completely unreliable.

If the Mount St. Helens eruption in 1980 was insufficient to impact the religious faith of Darwinism and uniformitarianism, God in His patience and grace designed yet another eruption from the same mountain, which occurred two years later in 1982. Not surprisingly, this second eruption received even less of an effort to connect the dots between the evidence presented and a young earth.

> This second eruption melted a thick snow pack, creating a sheet of water that quickly became a massive and destructive mudflow rushing down the mountain. The flow formed channels which cut through bedrock . . . individual canyons up to 140 feet deep were cut through the landslide debris and volcanic ash deposits.[13]

In one area, the rapid erosion created a one-fortieth scale model of the Grand Canyon.

According to the evolutionary timescale model, it took six million years for the Colorado River and other water flows off the plateaus to carve out the Grand Canyon. But the massive mudflow in 1982 carved out a little Grand Canyon in a matter of months. According to naturalist standards, it should have taken around 150,000 years for it to be created, but you can drive over there and see it today, just a few decades after its creation.

The erosion caused by the second eruption of Mount St. Helens also revealed very clearly the strata of sedimentary layers perfectly and symmetrically laid down in a matter of hours by the effects of the first eruption. Geologists were staggered that sediment layers 600 feet thick could be separated into distinct strata by water moving at 40 miles an hour. This was devastating to the conventional belief that it takes up to one million years for *each layer* of sediment to be laid down in rock layers. However, the layers around Mount St. Helens were laid down in a matter of months.

This evidence should have rewritten the textbooks. This volcano should have changed everything!

Unfortunately, there's been no rush to revise the geological standards of measurement and no acknowledgment in schoolbooks that the Grand Canyon could have been formed in one year. Science sites and resources still insist that it took 6 million years for the Grand Canyon to be carved out and that the formation of coal began 300 million years ago, on a planet billions of years old.

Why this persistence? It's because the world is always learning, but unable to come to the knowledge of the truth (2 Timothy 3:7).

AN OLD WARNING

For more than fifty years, a man named Harry owned and operated a lodge just a mile away from Mount St. Helens. He became a folk hero when he refused to evacuate the region, even though Mount St. Helens was giving all the signs of an imminent eruption. The warnings given by local authorities gave people plenty of time to evacuate, and all of Harry's neighbors heeded the warning to evacuate before 8:32 a.m. on May 18, 1980. But the old man refused to leave his home, telling reporters, "The mountain is a mile away; it ain't gonna hurt me!"

The eruption destroyed his lodge and buried everything, including Harry, 150 feet deep in avalanche debris . . . his body was never found.[14]

God issued a warning through Noah that judgment was coming—a global water catastrophe. Noah warned his world for 120 years of the coming judgment, as he built the ark that would preserve the lives of his family and the various animal kinds. His warnings were ignored, and the earth erupted and was overwhelmed by the great flood.

God has issued a warning through the apostle Peter that another judgment is coming—a catastrophe with fire. This warning has lasted now for nearly two thousand years. Peter warns:

> Know this first of all, that in the last days mockers will come with their mocking, following after their own

lusts, and saying, "Where is the promise of His coming? For ever since the fathers fell asleep, all continues just as it was from the beginning of creation." For when they maintain this, it escapes their notice that by the word of God the heavens existed long ago and the earth was formed out of water and by water, through which the world at that time was destroyed, being flooded with water. (2 Peter 3:3-6)

Notice carefully what these mockers do. They declare their faith in uniformitarianism—everything continues in the same way as it has always been since the beginning of time. In other words, nothing that hasn't happened before will happen in the future.

Peter used the global flood to challenge people's thinking that unusual things happen from time to time that disrupt any uniformity.

He warned about the next global judgment:

But the day of the Lord will come like a thief, in which the heavens will pass away with a roar and the elements will be destroyed with intense heat, and the earth and its works will be burned up. (2 Peter 3:10)

The next judgment will come not by water but by fire. Listen carefully, and take God at His word: the first world perished in a catastrophe, and the second world will perish as well.

The only safe place in Noah's day was inside the ark. Nobody beyond his own family took him up on the invitation. Similarly, there is only one escape from the next judgment—Jesus Christ. Those who take refuge in Him will arrive safely home.

One catastrophe happened in the past that changed the planet radically and the lives of those in it eternally.

Are you safe from the catastrophe to come?

CHAPTER TWO

A GOLDILOCKS WORLD

Nothing in creation leads believers to worship the creator God in absolute awe like the sky and the universe beyond.

Writing about the creation of the universe, the prophet Isaiah declared breathtaking truths every generation desperately needs to hear:

> Do you not know? Have you not heard? Has it not been declared to you from the beginning? Have you not understood from the foundations of the earth? It is He who sits above the circle of the earth, and its inhabitants are like grasshoppers, who stretches out the heavens like a curtain and spreads them out like a tent to dwell in . . . "To whom then will you liken Me that I would be his equal?" says the Holy One. Lift up your eyes on high and see who has created these stars, the One who leads forth their host by number, He calls them all by name; because of the greatness of His might and the strength of His power, not one of them is missing. (Isaiah 40:21-22, 25-26)

The author of Psalm 33 agreed with the prophet Isaiah—the powerful creative hands of God, seen in the grandeur of the heavens, lead us to worship Him in His majesty:

By the word of the Lord the heavens were made, and by the breath of His mouth all their host. He gathers the waters of the sea together as a heap; He lays up the deeps in storehouses. Let all the earth fear the Lord; let all the inhabitants of the world stand in awe of Him. For He spoke, and it was done; He commanded, and it stood fast. (Psalm 33:6–9)

Taking a tour of the heavens and the earth leads us to stand in awe of God.

Let's begin a tour—brief though it must be—by observing our home planet.

THE EARTH

Earth has a radius of about 3,960 miles and an equatorial circumference of about 24,901 miles. Spinning at over 1,000 miles per hour, the earth hurtles around the sun at 67,000 miles per hour . . . yes, you are moving really fast while reading this! In one year, we will travel approximately 584 million miles in our voyage around the sun.

At the beginning of a new year, many of us make resolutions. At the end of the year, we look back and usually have to admit that we broke most of them by the end of January.

But God resolved to keep His creation spinning (Genesis 8:22) until He interrupts it at the end of human history and creates a new earth and a new universe (Revelation 21:1).

You've probably read the children's fairy tale *Goldilocks and the Three Bears* in which a little girl named Goldilocks wanders into a cottage deep in the forest. Goldilocks finds the cottage empty, for its occupants, Papa Bear, Mama Bear, and Baby Bear, have left for a short walk in the forest while their porridge cools.

Feeling hungry and tired, Goldilocks tries everything out—the three bowls of porridge on the table, their three chairs, and even their three beds. With each of these things, she finds two options that don't work very well for her but eventually finds one that is "just right"—a bowl of porridge that is perfect to eat, a chair that perfectly suits her, and a bed that is perfectly comfortable.

Based on this children's story, the scientific community has coined the expression "The Goldilocks Zone" to refer to a region in space where conditions are "just right" for life—it is neither too hot nor too cold and allows for the existence of liquid water. Everything is just right!

It occurred to me that we live on a Goldilocks planet, where everything is "just right." Was it all an accident? Isaiah wrote, "He is the God who formed the earth and made it, He established it and did not create it a waste place, but formed it to be inhabited" (Isaiah 45:18).

Just as that porridge didn't evolve, God created the earth so that it supports life. The earth is not only the proper distance from the sun—not too hot and not too cold—but it also has "abundant liquid water, a breathable atmosphere, the perfectly sized sun to provide energy without killing life, and a perfectly sized moon to control the tides."[1]

An easily overlooked element in our Goldilocks planet is the earth's atmosphere, which has just the right amount and combination of gasses to prevent radical temperature swings that would otherwise fluctuate more than *a hundred degrees* every day.[2]

This stands in remarkable contrast with the earth's neighbors. For instance, on Venus, the earth's nearest twin in size, the atmosphere is made up of thick layers of carbon dioxide "converting the planet into a boiling inferno."[3] Mars lies in a "zone where liquid water might be possible," but the air pressure is so low, it causes water to boil away.[4]

The world has spent billions of dollars looking, unsuccessfully, for another planet that might have the same atmosphere as the earth. But the earth, just as Isaiah stated, is *uniquely* crafted to support life.

THE MOON

We tend to take the moon for granted, but it was the moon that led Sir Isaac Newton to his theory of gravity. I know we might think it was an apple falling on his head one afternoon; but in reality, it was the orbiting of the moon along with the effects of the moon upon the earth that led him to his "amazing insight into the fundamental laws of God's creation."[5]

After his amazing discoveries, Newton chided the unbelieving scientific world when he wrote, "Gravity explains the motions of the planets, but it cannot explain who set the planets in motion. God governs all things, and knows all that is or can be done."[6]

Scientists have spent some twenty billion dollars trying to explain how the moon *evolved*. The Bible tells us plainly in Genesis 1 that God created the moon on the fourth day of creation: He simply spoke it into existence by the breath of His mouth.[7]

How important is the moon? If the moon disappeared, the earth's axis would begin to wobble; the climate would become *The moon controls the tide* unstable; the planet would be locked into a permanent deep freeze or deep fry; and the ocean tides, which keep coastline waters from stagnating and drives currents around the world, would disappear.[8]

Without the moon, the earth would become a stagnating, stinking cesspool . . . goodbye, Goldilocks.

An article published by *National Geographic* showed that humans can survive for about forty-five days without food, seven days without water, ten minutes in temperatures above 300 degrees, and only three minutes without oxygen.[9]

This means that without perfect conditions, Adam and Eve would have died soon after God created them:

- They would have lasted forty-five days if there had not been fruit hanging from the branches and ready to eat.

- They would have lasted seven days, if there had not been fresh, clean water ready to drink.

- They would have lasted ten minutes if the earth's temperature was extremely high because the planet was too close to the sun.

- They would have lasted three minutes if no trees and plants were pumping out oxygen for them to breathe.

The question for the naturalist is this: Which one evolved *first?*

According to the Bible, everything was divinely created within a matter of days and in the right order so that life could exist on the earth. God spoke, and it was so—a Goldilocks planet for His prized creatures.

JUPITER

The largest planet in our solar system is Jupiter. Its volume is a thousand times greater than the earth's. Jupiter has been observed for two thousand years since it can be seen without the aid of telescopes. Ancient Babylonian astronomers used advanced geometry to understand the movements of planets and were able to track the path of Jupiter across the night sky.

Earth

In 1610, the Italian astronomer Galileo Galilei discovered four moons around Jupiter. Since then, more and more have been discovered. "Scientists now think Jupiter has a total of 67 moons."[10]

Jupiter

Radically different from earth, however, Jupiter is not inhabitable—and for several reasons. Jupiter is a gas planet, made mostly of hydrogen and helium. The core is surrounded by a liquid ocean of hydrogen. It appears there is no solid surface on which to walk.

Even if there were a solid surface, the atmosphere is extremely cold: minus 234 degrees Fahrenheit. The core is extremely hot: 43,000 degrees Fahrenheit, which is hotter than the surface of the sun.[11]

One of the most mysterious phenomena on Jupiter is what scientists call the "Great Red Spot," a massive storm that has been swirling on the planet for at least 150 years and probably much longer. While the largest and most powerful hurricane ever recorded on Earth spanned over 1,000 miles with winds of up to 200 miles per hour, this storm on Jupiter is twice as wide as the *earth* itself with winds reaching 400 miles per hour.[12]

Though beautiful and interesting, this gigantic planet cannot sustain life. Jupiter is not fit for Goldilocks.

THE SUN

Our sun is a star so huge it could fit one million earths inside it. In our Goldilocks system, the sun is just the right size and at just the right distance from the earth to keep life from freezing on our planet. Any alteration would be catastrophic for the earth since a single, typical flare from the sun's surface that sends warmth our way is equivalent to several nuclear bombs exploding at the same time.[13] Fortunately, the sun is 93 million miles away.

One of the puzzling and unique attributes of the sun is its stability. There's something unusual about its composition that allows for a very low amount of variation. And that's good!

Even though some have feared the sun could send out flares to fry us like bacon, God has designed the sun to warm the earth. According to the book of Revelation, the sun will still be around at the end of human history. So, until God finally judges mankind, the sun will continue to behave.

Sun

Earth

THE PISTOL STAR

If you think the sun is impressive—and it is—travel just outside the solar system, and you will discover a star much larger than the sun.

While the earth has a diameter of 7,926 miles, this huge star has a diameter of more than 100 *million* miles. The Pistol Star was discovered by the Hubble Space Telescope in the 1990s. It is so large you would be able to see it with the naked eye if other objects did not cloud the way.

The wind generated by the energy of this star is ten billion times stronger than our sun's. In fact, the Pistol Star generates more energy in *twenty seconds* than the sun does in one entire *year*.[14]

Fortunately, God placed this star 25,000 light-years away!

ANTARES

Though the Pistol Star is impressive, Antares is even more so.

Antares is a supergiant star that has a diameter of 600 million miles, or 700 times the sun's diameter.[15] Imagine, if the sun were the size of the head of a stickpin, Antares would be the size of a beach ball.

Are you feeling small yet?

For some perspective, if you were to fly in a plane traveling at an average speed of 500 miles per hour nonstop, you could circle the earth in two days. At the same speed, it would take you 20 days to circle Jupiter, and 200 days to make it around the sun! As for Antares, you wouldn't survive the trip since it would take longer than your entire life to circle the star just one time.

THE MILKY WAY

All these examples pale in comparison to the size of our galaxy. The Milky Way is usually considered to be at least 100,000 light-years across. It could be more.

One light-year is the distance a beam of light, moving in a straight line, can travel in a year. One light-year is approximately six trillion miles. But even if we could travel as fast as light—covering six trillion miles a year—it would still take us 100,000 years to go from one end of the Milky Way to the other.

That's how big our galaxy is . . . and beyond our galaxy are billions more!

So, how did the Milky Way come into existence? By the word of God's mouth. God didn't even lift a finger to create this vast system— He simply spoke and it came into existence.

> In the beginning God created the heavens and the earth. (Genesis 1:1)

LIFE OUTSIDE OUR GOLDILOCKS ZONE?

The vastness and apparent limitlessness of the universe have led many to postulate that there might be life beyond the earth. Surely, alien civilizations live outside our Goldilocks Zone, somewhere in this immeasurable universe.

In 2009, the Kepler telescope was launched into outer space to monitor 150,000 stars for evidence of orbiting planets and the possibility of other life-forms. After a decade of exploration that took it 90 million miles into space, the telescope ran out of fuel, ending the mission. None of the planets it observed have the unique features of earth that make life possible.

Still, extraterrestrial life is a growing conviction of our generation. The search for extraterrestrial intelligence (SETI) employs powerful radio telescopes to scan the heavens, not only for habitable planets but also "for signs of sophisticated extraterrestrial civilizations," according to Jill Tarter, cofounder of the SETI Institute.[16]

The idea of alien life comes largely from the belief in evolution. If you disregard the creation account of Genesis 1, our earth becomes just another planet created along with the rest of the universe from a big-bang explosion. The earth accidentally contains features that happened to create the puddle of goop that somehow initiated the development of atoms into complex cells. Consequently, other planets in the vast universe must share this same kind of goop. Maybe aliens even started evolving earlier than humans did and now have more sophisticated technology than we do. Maybe they even seeded our planet with life-forms.

The incredible odds somehow seem reasonable if the biblical account is denied.

According to Genesis 1:1, however, "God created the heavens [the universe] and the earth." The text implies special consideration to the earth. Furthermore, God informs us that the earth was uniquely designed to sustain life:

> For thus says the LORD, who created the heavens (He is the God who formed the earth and made it, He established it and did not create it a waste place, but formed it to be inhabited)." (Isaiah 45:18)

God created the heavenly bodies—billions of stars and planets—as *waste places*, that is, they are uninhabitable. Isaiah clearly states that Earth alone was *formed to be inhabited*.

While we're on the subject, the existence of aliens on other planets has at least two serious theological ramifications.

The first ramification relates to the doctrine of sin. The Bible reveals that the fall of Adam into sin brought about a curse, not just upon the human race and the physical earth, but also on *all* of creation. Everything God created has been corrupted and longs for redemption: "For we know that the *whole creation* groans and suffers the pains of childbirth together until now" (Romans 8:22). Therefore, that alien civilization out there has been corrupted by sin.

The second ramification relates to the doctrine of redemption. How does redemption take place in all of God's creation? The Creator became a member of the human race and died "once and for all" as a human man to raise a redeemed race of human beings who have repented of their sin and believed the gospel.[17] This means that of all the planets in the universe, it's the earth that God Himself visited, taking on the nature of the human race and redeeming forever those who trust in Him.

Therefore, this growing fascination with other worlds and alien races not only disregards the creation account, along with the prophet Isaiah's clear testimony; it also touches on gospel issues, denying the unique relationship between God and man, including the incarnation of God the Son into *human form.*

This leads me to two practical observations about the search for extraterrestrial life.

First, the possibility of life on other planets is often a thinly veiled hope that mankind can avoid a creator God. In other words, if life can be found on other worlds, then the Bible's focus on humans alone is prejudicial and its statements about God's unique creation of the earth for life is shown to be false. This means that whatever the Bible says about anything else, including a coming judgment, cannot be trusted.

If the universe is home to many other intelligent beings, unrelated to our creator God, then we really don't have to worry about God after all. And we certainly don't have to worry about a verse like Hebrews 9:27: "It is appointed for men to die once and after this comes judgment."

Second, mankind's passionate pursuit of alien life has become a replacement for passionately pursuing God.

In general, people feel a sense of loneliness and insignificance when they consider the size of the universe. But rather than look to God, many look for alien life to assure them they are not alone in the universe. Their pursuit ultimately leads to disappointment and despair, as it did for the great physicist Enrico Fermi, who lamented, "Where is everybody?"[18]

The Bible tells us we are *not alone* in the universe. God created the human race for fellowship with Him, and one day, we who know God will be with Him, and the universe will be our playground.

Unbelievers are pursuing alien civilizations with the hope that they'll be able to teach humans about the mysteries of the universe. Perhaps aliens will provide answers to the age-old questions of why we are here and where we came from and where we're going. They might even have advanced medical knowledge that would allow us to live longer or never get sick or perhaps not even have to die.

For believers, Scripture answers those crucial questions and gives us hope. God gives us purpose and identity as we passionately pursue Him through His Word. God will one day heal all our diseases, and we will live forever in newly glorified, eternal, perfected bodies that never give out or wear out.

If given a choice, however, the average person in our generation would prefer an alien race rather than God provide answers to these questions.

In an interview in the 2008 movie *Expelled*, evolutionary biologist and author Richard Dawkins advanced the "intriguing possibility" (as he called it) that highly evolved aliens "seeded" life on the earth. In other words, he concedes that intelligent design might account for life on the earth, but he prefers that intelligent design to be aliens instead of God.[19]

There are trillions upon trillions of stars and planets in billions of galaxies. The farther out we look, the farther out the universe stretches. But the farther out we look, the more often we're reminded that there is no life outside this Goldilocks planet—*Earth*. Even in our own relatively small galaxy, the Milky Way, there is only one Goldilocks planet and one Goldilocks Zone.

There is a reason for that.

IS GOD A SHOW-OFF?

Why did God make the universe so vast? Isaiah explained why:

> Lift up your eyes on high and see who has created these stars, the One who leads forth their host by number, He calls them all by name; because of the greatness of His might and the strength of His power, not one of them is missing. (Isaiah 40:26)

The Lord of the universe asks us to look up and become amazed and in awe of His power, grace, care, and attention over all of creation. He cares for those planets and stars so much that He has given a name to each one of them. And if He has given chunks of rock and gas that kind of attention, imagine the attention He has given to *you*, one who has been created eternally in His image?

We might be small, but we are prized, loved, pursued, redeemed, directed, longed for, and looked after by our creator God. He is aware of us, loves us, and invites us to walk with Him and talk to Him through faith in His Son, Jesus Christ, who is our Savior *and* Creator.

This is the gospel: The Creator left His throne above the universe and became one of us in order to die for us and pay the penalty for our sin and to defeat death and the grave at His resurrection. Now He is seated above the universe, promising those of us who believe in Him a future that defies our imagination.

So, Christian, don't shrink your life down to living for yourself, sin, or this planet. Never measure the significance of your life by what you can get, drive, wear, spend, store in your attic, or collect in your garage as you live ever so briefly on this tiny little planet.

You were created for so much more. You are heading for an incredible future![20] You will reign with all other followers of Christ as co-regents with Jesus Christ in His coming kingdom (2 Timothy 2:12).

This was the amazing conclusion of the psalmist David:

> When I consider Your heavens, the work of Your fingers, the moon and the stars, which You have ordained; what is man that You take thought of him, and the son of man that You care for him? . . . O Lord, our Lord, how majestic is Your name in all the earth! (Psalm 8:3-4, 9)

To think that God is mindful of you and me . . . wow!

He knows our names, too. Because of our redemption through Christ, God has written our names in the Lamb's Book of Life (Revelation 21:27).

God created the Goldilocks world in which we live now, but nothing compares to the Goldilocks future He has reserved for those who belong to Him!

CHAPTER THREE

THE ORIGINAL
JUNGLE BOOK

F ew things capture our fascination, wonder, curiosity, and amazement like a good story involving wild animals, especially big ones. The animal kingdom inspires awe and fascination.

One of the most overlooked marvels of the Bible is that it introduces us to hundreds of different kinds of animals, including crocodiles, cheetahs, lions, bears, snakes, frogs, deer, antelope, badgers, locusts, foxes, wolves, fish, sheep, dogs, *and* dinosaurs.

The Bible is the original *Jungle Book*!

Most of the animals mentioned in the creation account of Genesis and revealed throughout the Bible are understood to be real and contemporary with the Bible's authors. Nobody contests the existence of crocodiles, cheetahs, and panthers in Bible times. But any suggestion that dinosaurs lived alongside these animals *and* human beings is met with disbelief and ridicule.

DINOSAURS: YESTERDAY AND TOMORROW

No animals have captured people's fascination quite like the dinosaurs. Undoubtedly, this is due in part to the enormous size of some of them. But dinosaurs, more than any other creatures, have been used by evolutionists to indoctrinate generations of children and adults in the belief that the earth must be millions of years old.

There is still mystery surrounding the dinosaurs, and this exists *because* the biblical record has long been abandoned. The Bible, which is the history book of the universe and the prophecy book of a future universe, is ignored.[1]

According to God, the only *eyewitness* at the beginning of the universe, the dinosaurs and all other land animals were created on the sixth day of creation. Later that same day, God created the first human beings, Adam and Eve.

The entire universe was created with mature features in place so that it would immediately function and sustain life on this planet. This means the stars were created with their light already speeding up to provide light to the earth, although they were billions of light-years away; trees were created mature and already bearing leaves and fruit; the grass was already rich and luxuriant, ready for the land animals that would be created to immediately graze upon it. Likewise, Adam and Eve were created, not as embryos, but as physically mature adults— walking, talking, planning, eating, working, and worshipping God.

The world they entered was vastly different from our world today. It was a "fearless age," marked by the absence of fear between humans and animals.[2] Adam and Eve and all the animals were originally herbivores:

The T-Rex was originally vegetarian!

> God said, "Behold, I have given you every plant yielding seed that is on the surface of all the earth, and every tree which has fruit yielding seed; it shall be food for you; and to every beast of the earth and to every bird of the sky and to every thing that moves on the earth which has life, I have given every green plant for food"; and it was so. God saw all that He had made, and behold, it was very good. And there was evening and there was morning, the sixth day. (Genesis 1:29-31)

> In other words, dinosaurs, including the T-rex, were not carnivores when God created them. Along with every other animal, they were vegetarians.

Some argue that the teeth of the T-rex prove otherwise—that meat was its main diet. Appearances, however, can be deceiving.

The panda bear, for instance, has sharp teeth like those of a meat eater, but it eats bamboo. The marine iguana looks like a savage meat eater with rows of very sharp teeth, but it is vegetarian.

Animals we now know as predators were originally designed by God to be satisfied with plant life. And they remained that way until the fall of Adam and Eve into sin.

A recent discovery in India provides an unusual glimpse at the dinosaur's diet. After carefully studying fossilized dinosaur dung, scientists found that the diet of the dinosaur included several different types of *grass*.[3]

Everything changed, however, with the intrusion of sin into the created world. Among the many changes recorded in the Bible, several animal species, including some dinosaurs, became predators. The once vegetarian T-rex stopped eating celery and began to eat other animals—and human beings. The reason dinosaur bones and human bones are not found near each other is obvious: people simply didn't live around them.

Sin not only brought spiritual corruption to Adam and Eve and all mankind ever since; it also distorted nature and the animal kingdom. Sin transformed the animal kingdom into a very brutal realm. There is no mercy between species. It's called a *food chain* for a reason.

Mankind had to deal with a very powerful threat until the predatory dinosaurs disappeared, like many other species. However, this did not occur 65 million years ago but relatively recently.

One historical account of life in England dated to AD 1405, only 600 years ago, reads:

> Close to the town of Bures, near Sudbury, there has lately appeared, to the great hurt of the countryside, a beast, vast in body, with a crested head, teeth like a saw, and a tail extending to an enormous length.[4]

Unfortunately, nobody had a camera.

Ever since the fall of man, it has generally held true that the bigger you are, the more advantageous your position on the food chain. To this day, the animal kingdom is bristling with tension, fear, and danger.

If you observe the birds, for example, you will notice that they are always on high alert, looking this way and that. Before dipping down into the birdbath, they frantically look everywhere. Even when they land at the feeder to get a seed, they remain on high alert, fearful of being attacked by a bigger bird who wants that food. As soon as a mockingbird flies in, all the finches and bluebirds take off. When a hawk starts crying out overhead, the mockingbird takes cover.

According to the *original* Jungle Book, God's Word, such fear among animals is the result of sin. When mankind fell, the natural world fell as well.

Paul wrote that "through one man sin entered into the world, and death through sin" (Romans 5:12). Sin entered the *world*, not just the human race. The entire world was affected and corrupted.

Paul explained further:

> For the creation was subjected to futility, not willingly, but because of Him who subjected it, in hope that the creation itself also will be set free from its slavery to corruption into the freedom of the glory of the children of God. For we know that the whole creation groans and suffers the pains of childbirth together until now. (Romans 8:20-22)

All creation longs for the glory of the coming kingdom and the reign of Christ on earth in the millennium. At that time the animal kingdom will return to the days of Eden.

Isaiah described this amazing reversal in the animal world during Christ's kingdom:

> And the wolf will dwell with the lamb, and the leopard will lie down with the young goat, and the calf and the young lion and the fatling together; and a little boy will lead them. Also the cow and the bear will graze, their

young will lie down together, and the lion will eat straw like the ox. The nursing child will play by the hole of the cobra, and the weaned child will put his hand on the viper's den. They will not hurt or destroy in all My holy mountain, for the earth will be full of the knowledge of the LORD as the waters cover the sea. (Isaiah 11:6-9)

If we begin with the biblical record of beginnings, much of the mystery of the past is solved—including the dinosaurs. On the other hand, the mystery only intensifies when we abandon Scripture and accept the evolutionary speculations that dinosaurs eventually evolved from amphibians millions of years ago.

Scientific speculations sometimes prove embarrassing. In the 1990s, explorers found elephants in Nepal that have many features of mammoths, a species considered to have gone extinct four thousand years ago. Explorers in the jungles of the Congo encountered what they described as dinosaur-like animals.[5] Even more interesting are the cave paintings by Native Americans that depict people hunting mammoths *and* dinosaurs.

Unfortunately, science textbooks don't like being updated. Though they might include the drawings of people hunting mammoths, any artistic evidence that dinosaurs and humans were contemporaries is conveniently left out. Dinosaurs simply *have* to be millions of years old for evolutionary speculations to remain intact.

But are dinosaurs really that old?

In 2005, a team of scientists led by paleontologist Mary Schweitzer published a paper in which they described an unusual find. In the innermost parts of the fossilized femur of a T-rex, somehow sealed off from fossilizing fluids, they found intact blood vessels and red blood cells.

The paper produced an uproar in the scientific community. If the T-rex was 65 million years old, blood vessels and soft tissue would have long since disintegrated.

The scientific world immediately attacked Mary Schweitzer's conclusions, arguing that the blood vessels were film created by bacteria and that bacterial residue created only what looked like red blood cells. Schweitzer's findings were written off completely.

Then in 2009, Schweitzer and her team produced a new paper based on their study of the bones of a duck-billed dinosaur, whose age was supposedly 80 million years. Once again, they found a host of soft-tissue structures, proteins, hemoglobin, and bone-forming cells. This time Schweitzer and her team allowed multiple, independent laboratories to test their findings.

The discovery of soft tissue was real.[6]

Concluding that the soft tissue somehow was preserved for 80 million years, researchers are now left with determining the mechanism by which this preservation took place. A more obvious conclusion is that the bones, in fact, are not 80 million years old but only a few thousand years old, which is in harmony with God's History Book.

DINOSAURS: VISUAL AIDS FOR SUFFERING SERVANTS

There are at least three reasons why the biblical teaching that dinosaurs and humans lived at the same time is so important.

1. The truthfulness of the eyewitness account of creation depends on whether all land animals were, in fact, created on the sixth day along with Adam and Eve, as stated in Genesis 1:24-31.

2. If the record of creation is false, then not only is the biblical description of the ancient world untrue but the biblical description of the *future* world is equally untrue.

3. If dinosaurs became extinct millions of years before human beings existed or evolved, one of the most amazing evidences that God cares about us when we suffer is *lost*.

The book of Job is filled with references to the universe, creation, and the animal kingdom. In fact, "the book of Job contains more modern scientific insights than any other book of the Bible."[7]

Near the end of Job's immense suffering, God breaks His silence and takes His servant on a tour through the created world. At the end of the tour, God shows Job the two largest animals ever created:

the largest sea animal, the *leviathan*, and the largest land animal, the *behemoth*, which matches the description of a sauropod dinosaur. The word *dinosaur* was coined in 1841 by Sir Richard Owen and thus does not appear in the Bible.[8]

Some interpreters have identified the behemoth as a water buffalo, a rhinoceros, or a hippopotamus. However, these creatures do not match the biblical description of the behemoth.

God wants to show His *power* in creation in order to bring comfort to Job, and there is no better example of His power than a sauropod dinosaur. Skeletal remains of sauropod dinosaurs demonstrate that they were massive creatures, the

Was this creature the behemoth?

largest of which weighed more than 100 metric tons and stretched between 80 to 130 feet long and stood 60 feet high.

God's description leaves little doubt it is such a creature that He points out for Job to observe:

> "Behold now, Behemoth, which I made as well as you; he eats grass like an ox. Behold now, his strength in his loins and his power in the muscles of his belly. He bends his tail like a cedar; the sinews of his thighs are knit together. His bones are tubes of bronze; his limbs are like bars of iron. He is the first of the ways of God." (Job 40:15-19)

This description rules out the elephant and the hippo, whose tails resemble a piece of string, not cedar trees.

The words "he is the first of the ways of God" does not mean he is the first animal God created but that he is first in size and strength. He is the biggest land creature God ever created.

God essentially says to Job: "I knew how to put that massive creature together, just like I knew how to put *you* together."

Through this amazing creature, God teaches Job two lessons.

Mankind Is Frail and His Abilities Are Unimpressive

By showing this dinosaur to Job, God effectively puts him in his place. In the presence of this massive creature that Job could behold with his own eyes, he must have felt utterly powerless and unimpressive.

Awesome creatures remind us of how small, frail, and dependent we are on the power of God. This viewing session of the sauropod dinosaur is meant to humble Job . . . and all of us. We should think twice before challenging the Creator who formed these monstrous creatures.[9]

God Is Powerful and His Plans Are Unstoppable

At the end of his visual tour, Job says to God, "I know that You can do all things" (Job 42:2). In other words, "If you can create these massive creatures, you can create *anything*."

Job continues: "No purpose of Yours can be thwarted" (Job 42:2). Job realizes that God is not only powerful, but His purposes are unstoppable.

This massive creature served as a living illustration to Job that God had been in control over everything, *including* Job's own suffering.

Just like Job, we can take comfort in God's control over the events of our own lives, whether delightful or discouraging. When we marvel at the Creator's handiwork, we begin to feel, once again, the touch of the Creator's hand.[10]

*****

In his book *The Great House of God*, Max Lucado writes about the effect of creation on the believer:

> I've seen you searching for a gift. I've seen you stalking the malls and walking the aisles . . . I'm talking about that extra-special person and that extra-special gift. I'm talking about stashing away a few dollars a month out of

the grocery money to buy him some lizard-skin boots; staring at a thousand rings to find her the best diamond; staying up all night Christmas Eve, assembling the new bicycle. Why do you do it? You do it so the eyes will pop. You do it so the heart will stop. You do it so the jaw will drop. You do it to hear those words of disbelief, "You did this for *me?*"

That's why you do it. And that is why God did it. Next time a sunrise steals your breath or a meadow of flowers leaves you speechless, remain that way. Say nothing and listen as heaven whispers, "Do you like it? I did it just for you."[11]

God gave us such an amazing creation so that we would be sustained by it, cultivate it, study it, learn from it, marvel at it, and then give to the Creator our highest compliments and glory.

During days of deepest valleys and darkest seasons, look around. Take a good look at what God has created. Then return to Him your deepest confidence and trust.

Marvel at creation . . . then worship your Creator!

CHAPTER FOUR

TAUGHT BY A FOREST OF TREES

The current population of the world is around 8 billion people, soon to be 9 billion. Most of the oxygen for 16 billion sets of lungs is produced by trees. Specialists were concerned about the number of trees alive and estimated that there were only 400 billion trees providing oxygen for a growing population. Environmentalists feared this number was insufficient to produce the oxygen necessary for the world's growing population, especially since one billion trees were being cut down every year. Specialists had further calculated that one mature tree produced, in one year, the oxygen necessary for two people to inhale in that given year. They had reason, so they said, for sounding the alarm.

So in 2013, experts working with the School of Forestry and Environmental Sciences at Yale University launched an aggressive global program to plant one billion trees. The Yale team also conducted the first ever comprehensive survey to determine how many trees there were on the planet. An exact census had never been conducted before.

With the help of national forest inventories and newly advanced satellite imaging, the team spent two years studying all the available data. Finally, in 2015 the environmentalist world was embarrassingly stunned with the discovery that there are more than three *trillion* living trees on the earth. That amounted to more than four hundred trees per person.[1]

We are *not* running short of trees, and we're *not* running out of oxygen.

But let's not take the subject of trees for granted. They happen to declare the creative genius and glory of our creator God.

TREES ARE MARVELS OF GOD'S CREATION

Botanists estimate there are at least 60,000 tree species in the world.[2] But where did the trees—or even wood itself—originally come from?

The answer eludes evolutionists. They are forced to admit their lack of knowledge on this matter, as did evolutionist Elizabeth Stacy from the University of Hawaii:

> We know next to nothing about how they got here.
> . . . Trees form the backbone of our forests, and are eco-
> logically and economically important, yet we don't know
> much about how speciation happens in trees.[3]

The fossil record actually sheds much light on the subject, when paired with the Genesis account of creation.

The fossil evidence reveals dinosaurs wandered among the oak, willow, and magnolia trees. New research has proven that the genome of spruces, pines, and fir trees have hardly changed at all since the days of the dinosaurs.[4]

One example is the Wollemi pine tree, which is often called "the dinosaur tree." Ironically, this tree was discovered alive and well in Australia in 1994. Known previously only through fossils, the tree was believed to have become extinct 150 million years ago, yet it was discovered living and growing, showing no evolutionary changes when compared to the fossils, which were presumed to be millions of years old.[5] Maybe that's because trees didn't *evolve!*

Trees puzzle evolutionists. For them, the origin of wood is unknown and they can't quite figure out how, where, and when the first tree came to be.

Wollemi Pine Tree –
no evidence of evolution

Believers, on the other hand, accept the eyewitness account of God, who informs us that trees were created by His verbal and creative command on the third day of the creation week. On that fruitful day, God spoke into existence vegetation, which included trees: "Then God said, 'Let the earth sprout vegetation, plants yielding seed, and fruit trees on the earth bearing fruit after their kind with seed in them'" (Genesis 1:11).

The language of this creative act indicates that God commanded into existence a fully mature system with trees *already* bearing fruit. God spoke into existence a completely developed creation, which would have been necessary for animals and mankind to survive.

Skeptics often argue that if the biblical account is accurate, then it makes God deceptive since He created things having the appearance of being older than they actually were. The answer to that charge is simple: This isn't deceptive because God Himself tells us up front in the creation account that His creation was immediate and supernatural and necessary to function properly from the outset. Full-grown fruit trees had to be present immediately to provide food and produce oxygen for the animal kingdom and the human race, which were created just three days later.

Trees already bearing fruit

The Creator suddenly created the earth's trees. And the more we discover about them, the more amazing is the miracle of their creation.

Trees are marvelous *externally*.

The shape of a tree is extremely important for its survival. It's not a random design. The superior rounded fashion allows it to bend and flex with the wind in all directions yet at the same time support the crown of branches and leaves with maximum strength (our telephone poles, by the way, follow the same pattern).

While God designed most living things to breathe in oxygen and breathe out carbon dioxide as a waste product, trees, on the other hand, absorb carbon dioxide from the atmosphere and breathe out oxygen. Without them, we can't survive.

Researchers are still discovering much about what goes on below the ground as well. The old view was that trees competed in a life-and-death struggle for limited light and resources, but current research is learning that trees assist each other.[6]

For instance, when a young sapling springs up in the shade of a thick forest, older trees don't resist its presence but through their roots share nutrients with the sapling. Older trees even change their root structure to make room for the roots of younger trees.[7]

God has designed older trees to assist younger trees—and there's a spiritual lesson for us in that natural phenomenon.

Trees are marvelous *internally* too.

Trees have no skeleton to provide support and strength, but inside them are cells with trillions of robust cell walls that give strength to the whole organism. These trillions of cell walls make up the wood of the tree.

The tree is an incredible factory where the work never stops. A vascular system in the tree, made up of tube-like systems, draws an enormous amount of water from the roots to the leaves and then sends food, crafted by the leaves, back down to the roots.

Some trees even have a defense system against being overeaten by animals: they produce chemicals that make their leaves taste bad. For instance, as a hungry insect salivates on certain elm trees, the trees chemically reproduce the saliva and emit that chemical into the air. The odor alerts predators who like to eat that particular insect, prompting them to come flying in to eat the invading creature![8]

Trees even communicate among themselves through microscopic tubes connecting the roots of different trees. Electrical impulses are constantly passing through the nerve-like cells of these networks from root tip to root tip, broadcasting everything from drought conditions to predator attacks. This sophisticated network below a forest of trees has been called the "underground internet" and the "wood wide web."[9]

Trees are marvels of God's creation.

TREES ARE METAPHORS FOR GODLY BELIEVERS

Time after time, the authors of Scripture refer to trees as illustrations of godly believers. The psalmist wrote:

> Blessed is the man... [whose] delight is in the law of the LORD, and in His law he meditates day and night. He will be like a tree firmly planted by streams of water, which yields its fruit in its season and its leaf does not wither; and in whatever he does, he prospers. (Psalm 1:1-3)

The prophet Jeremiah agreed when he wrote:

> Blessed is the man who trusts in the LORD and whose trust is the LORD. For he will be like a tree planted by the water, that extends its roots by a stream and will not fear when the heat comes; but its leaves will be green, and it will not be anxious in a year of drought nor cease to yield fruit. (Jeremiah 17:7-8)

Both the psalmist and the prophet invite us to study a tree. The best parts of the life of a tree are analogous to the best parts of our lives when we're rooted in relationship with the Lord.

In the New Testament, God commands older believers in the faith to assist younger ones. Just as older trees assist younger trees in their development, older believers have the responsibility to teach younger believers—older women teaching younger women and older men teaching younger men (Titus 2:2-8).

Growth. Strength. Productivity. Security. Stability. Perseverance to withstand adversity. Fruitfulness. These are some of the characteristics of a believer who is tree-like—rooted in the confidence of the character of God.

TREES ARE MESSENGERS OF WARNINGS AND PROMISES

Trees of Warning

On one occasion, Jesus Christ used a fruitless fig tree to illustrate the fruitlessness of that current generation of Israelites. Israel was empty spiritually, so by cursing the fig tree, Jesus was pronouncing judgment on the nation (Matthew 21:19).

One of the fearful effects of judgment that will fall on the human race after the rapture of the church involves trees.

Why did Jesus curse the fig tree?

During that future tribulation period, God will pour out His wrath on the earth. Among many other judgments, He will bombard the planet with hail and fire, so that one-third of all the trees will be destroyed (Revelation 8:7). Near the end of the tribulation, hailstones will rain down on earth, each hailstone weighing around one hundred pounds (Revelation 16:21). The largest hailstones recorded in recent history weighed about two pounds. Imagine hundred-pound hailstones! Earthquakes will accompany these horrific firestorms and hailstorms.

Throughout history, and to this day, people have worshipped nature, defying the creator God by elevating nature above everything and everyone. The instrument God will use to unleash His wrath in the end-time tribulation will be nature. It's as if God will say, "You've always wanted Mother Nature, so I'll give you Mother Nature!" Imagine one *trillion* trees destroyed in a matter of days!

As God wipes out one-third of the trees on the planet, oxygen will be reduced drastically in much of the world. Breathing difficulty may be a very real part of the horrific conditions on earth as the wrath of God is unleashed during the seven-year tribulation.

One of the final warnings we read about with regard to the end of human history involves trees. But the very *first* warning in all of human history also involved a tree. We can call it *the tree of pride*:

> The LORD God commanded the man, saying, "From any tree of the garden you may eat freely; but from the tree of the knowledge of good and evil you shall not eat, for in the day that you eat from it you will surely die." (Genesis 2:16-17)

Following the alluring temptation of Satan to eat from that tree and become as wise as God, the woman took the initiative in her independence and pride. And Adam soon followed in his defiant pride.

As sin entered the world. Adam and Eve, who would have lived forever in that perfect condition had they not rebelled against the Creator, began to die. Cells in their bodies died; their physical condition began to be affected by an aging process they'd never experienced before.

God placed that tree in the garden so that Adam and Eve, though innocent by nature, had a choice to make: pride or humility, obedience or defiance.

There they were in the garden of Eden, or garden of Delight. They were allowed to eat from any tree they liked, except for this one. What would their priority be? Would it be fellowship with God, worship of God, and obedience to God?

The couple chose, instead, self-willed, self-promoting, and self-exalting sin. Ultimately, this meant defying, denying, and despising God.

The judgment was death. They were immediately subjected to physical decay and ultimately death, and spiritually they were immediately separated from the Creator. They were also physically cast out of the garden.

Trees of Promise

Before they were expelled from the garden of Delight, where they had enjoyed an intimate relationship with God, Adam and Eve received the promise of a coming Deliverer. Though the Deliverer would suffer and die, He would crush Satan and deliver sinners from eternal punishment.

Along with this promise of a Deliverer came yet another tree—*the tree of pardon.*

The apostle Paul wrote: "Christ redeemed us from the curse of the Law, having become a curse for us—for it is written, 'Cursed is everyone who hangs on a tree'" (Galatians 3:13).

In ancient Judaism, a criminal worthy of the death penalty was typically stoned to death and then tied up or hung from a post or tree. His body would hang until sunset as a visible statement that he had been judged by the law and rejected by God (Deuteronomy 21:22-23). The criminal was not rejected *because* he hung from a tree; he hung from a tree as a sign that he had been rejected by God.

The tree of Pardon

Jesus Christ took upon Himself our sins and willingly hung on a tree. While on the tree of pardon, the Son of God was rejected by God the Father. Christ Jesus bore such rejection so that sinners could be accepted by God the Father through faith in Christ.

There remains, however, another tree that appears at the very end of the biblical revelation. It's *the tree of promise,* which is connected to the believer's eternal hope.

In his vision of the end times, the apostle John described the Celestial City in Revelation 21–22. He explained that on either side of the river of life that cascades down from the throne of God, there is an orchard of trees adorning the main boulevard of the Holy City.

Interestingly, the only vegetation given special mention in heaven is a tree—the tree of life:

> Then he showed me a river of the water of life, clear as crystal, coming from the throne of God and of the Lamb, in the middle of its street. On either side of the

river was the tree of life, bearing twelve kinds of fruit, yielding its fruit every month; and the leaves of the tree were for the healing of the nations. (Revelation 22:1-2)

There will be trees in the New Jerusalem, and they will bear fruit. God will alter the natural process of fruit production so that these trees will have twelve kinds, or crops, of fruit, and it will yield a fresh crop every month. This is the tree of promise, also known as the Tree of Life.

Three Trees, One Invitation

The first tree, in the garden, witnessed the sin of mankind and the curse of sin on the human race. The second tree, on Calvary, witnessed the Savior of mankind and the curse borne in His own body on that tree. The third tree, in heaven, will witness the splendor of heaven forever.

The tree of pride can be solved only by the tree of pardon. Those who have gone to this second tree of pardon will enjoy the final tree—which grows in orchards along heaven's river of life.

There is no access to the tree of life without first kneeling at the tree of pardon—the cross of Jesus Christ.

Have you come by faith to that tree?

CHAPTER FIVE

NATURE GONE WILD

It was September 1996 when Hurricane Fran made its landfall near Cape Fear, North Carolina. The winds reached gusts of 115 miles per hour. Twenty-seven deaths were attributed to the storm, and damages reached $5 billion.

Nine years later, Hurricane Katrina struck the Gulf Coast. One of the deadliest and most destructive hurricanes to ever hit the United States, the sustained winds of this Category 5 storm reached 175 miles per hour at its peak. More than 1,800 people died according to some estimates, and damages exceeded $125 billion!

Every year people brace for the next hurricane and the devastation it brings.

Whether it's a landslide, a hurricane, a blizzard, a tornado, a flood, or an earthquake, whenever nature goes wild, people—sometimes many, many people—are negatively affected. And even those who are not directly affected—believers and unbelievers alike—are disturbed by the destruction and death caused by these natural phenomena.

What does Scripture teach regarding the wild side of nature? Where do natural disasters come from, why do they occur, and what can they possibly teach us?

Mankind has attempted to answer the question of hurricanes and storms for thousands of years. In Greek mythology, the god Aeolus was considered the divine keeper of the winds and the king of a floating island called Aeolia. Aeolus was in charge of keeping the violent storm winds locked away on his island. For the most part, he did a good job, unless other gods became angry with mankind and convinced Aeolus to let the winds loose to wreak havoc on the human race.[1] So, whenever the land was devastated by hurricanes, the Greek world assumed Aeolus was the culprit.

Just recently, a satellite with special equipment capable of transmitting precise wind-profile observations from around the globe was launched. It's the first satellite ever designed with this capability, and it's been named *Aeolus*, after the god who was ruler of the wind.[2] Surely the gods need to be recognized, right?

The Vikings had a storm god named *Odin*. Because he was often pictured along with wolves and dogs, these animals became symbols of the wind.

The Vikings also believed that witches supposedly rode their brooms high in the air, stirring up the rain clouds. They were often pictured with black cats, which in ancient times became the animal symbol for heavy rain and ominous storms. The expression "raining cats and dogs" may have emerged from the superstition that high winds and torrential rain were the work of gods and witches conspiring together.[3]

Most often, God is blamed for the latest natural disaster. After one recent storm, a journalist brazenly stated, "If this world is the product of intelligent design, then the Designer has some explaining to do."[4]

Is God in control over natural disasters?

What exactly should we say to someone who has suffered loss in a hurricane? What should we say to someone like Job and his wife, who lost all ten of their children after a tornado came out of nowhere and leveled the house where all the grown children were enjoying a birthday party? Was God, in any way, involved?

The word *storm* appears in the Bible forty times—thirty-five times in the Old Testament and five times in the New Testament. In none of these occurrences does the Bible even hint that somehow the storm slipped out of God's control.

Indeed, God is described unfailingly throughout Scripture as sovereign and in complete control over nature, even when it might seem that nature has gone wild. This is clearly revealed in a psalm of praise:

> He sends forth His command to the earth; His word runs very swiftly. He gives snow like wool; He scatters the frost like ashes. He casts forth His ice as fragments; who can stand before His cold? He sends forth His word and melts them; He causes His wind to blow and the waters to flow. (Psalm 147:15-18)

Many Christians believe God has *nothing* to do with natural disasters—they assume that God simply allows nature to take its course and then tries to make something good out of it. On the other hand, these same Christians pray for sunshine on their outdoor wedding.

After a recent earthquake in California, a group of pastors met for a prayer breakfast. They talked about the disaster and its terrible aftermath and then came to the conclusion that God had nothing to do with it. Ironically, when one of the pastors concluded the meeting with a prayer, he thanked God for the *timing* of the earthquake, which had taken place at five o'clock in the morning when there were few cars on the highway and the sidewalks of the city were empty. When he finished his prayer, all his colleagues echoed "Amen!"[5] How do you thank God for timing the earthquake if He had no control over it?

That God has the weather under control is especially evident in the Gospels. On one occasion, Jesus was with His disciples on a boat in the middle of the Sea of Galilee. While a storm raged, the Lord slept. After being awakened by the disciples, who were terrified, Jesus displayed His power over nature by saying to the windstorm and the waves crashing into the boat, "Hush, be still." The result was immediate: "And the wind died down and it became perfectly calm" (Mark 4:39). The reaction of the disciples was only natural. They said to one another: "Who then is this, that even the wind and the sea obey Him?" (verse 41). The answer is obvious: Only God can control the forces of nature, and that's exactly who Jesus was proving He was.

According to the biblical revelation, God's good purposes are carried out even through the sorrow, suffering, pain, and death produced by natural disasters. The prophet Nahum introduces God as One who is in the hurricane and in the storm (Nahum 1:3). God Himself declared, "The One forming light and creating darkness, causing well-being and creating calamity; I am the LORD who does all these" (Isaiah 45:7).

While well-meaning Christians try to get God off the hook by denying His involvement in natural disasters, God takes responsibility for them. This, in fact, is the *only* explanation that gives hope to any of us. Disasters aren't random, meaningless, or purposeless events out of God's control. God didn't disappear, mess things up, or turn His back on us. God alone knows His purpose in it, and He will one day reveal it.

This is our confidence as believers: This is *His* universe, and that is *His* storm, *His* lightning, and *His* flood, just as it is *His* sunshine, *His* quiet breeze, and *His* beautiful creatures of earth!

Is God in control of natural disasters? Noah certainly hoped so as he floated in the ark during the global flood. Is God in control of hungry predators? That's the explanation Daniel gave King Darius the morning after surviving a night in the lions' den (Daniel 6:21-22). Was God in control of that huge fish that swallowed Jonah alive? If Jonah didn't believe that, he never would have bothered praying while in the belly of the fish (Jonah 2).

If God can *command* the natural world, He's in *control* of the natural world.

Even when everything looks like chaos and nature appears to be running wild, God is ultimately in control. And this gives us hope, confidence, and rest in the sovereign plan of God.

With this perspective, we can follow the example of the person who said, "I have learned to kiss the wave that throws me against the Rock of Ages."[6]

What lessons do storms and natural disasters teach believers?

WISE LESSONS FROM WILD NATURE

Natural Disasters Reveal the Frailty of Life

Natural disasters reveal how utterly dependent we are on God for the basic things of life. To this day, even though there continues to be much talk about seeding clouds, human beings simply can't control the weather.

Years ago, hundreds of people held hands and prayed in downtown Atlanta, just outside the state capitol

How dependent are we on Christ?

building. Water levels were at an all-time low, and restrictions put in place months earlier were not enough to compensate for the dwindling supply.

Georgia's governor risked mockery and anger by calling for a public prayer meeting. He said, "I'm here today to appeal to you and to all Georgians and to all people who believe in the power of prayer to ask God to shower our state, our region, our nation with the blessings of water."[7]

A few years later, the governor of Texas made an even bolder statement by calling for an all-day prayer event in Houston. He invited his fellow governors to join him at the event, stating:

> Right now, America is in crisis: we have been besieged by financial debt, terrorism, and a multitude of natural disasters. As a nation, we must come together and call upon Jesus to guide us through unprecedented struggles, and thank Him for the blessings we so richly enjoy.[8]

This is only fitting since every raindrop, icicle, tornado, and hurricane is an actor in God's drama of the ages. In the meantime, trouble reminds us of the frailty of life and the powerlessness of any of us to produce one raindrop or, for that matter, to *stop* one raindrop from falling.

Natural disasters are God's way of asking us, "Who do you think you are?" They humble us in reverence before our Creator and force us to acknowledge that Someone greater than us is in control.

Natural Disasters Remind Us to Remain Alert and Walk Closely with the Lord

The apostle Peter warns us: "Be on the alert. Your adversary, the devil, prowls around like a roaring lion, seeking someone to devour" (1 Peter 5:8). We never know when a spiritual battle will arise, so we must stay on high alert.

This is where a hurricane is different from any spiritual battle we face. With a hurricane, we might have several days of advance warning. We are given ample opportunity to evacuate the danger zone. Meteorologists become our favorite people.

As the storm moves closer and closer, there is an abundance of reporting on the results from high-tech equipment that is tracking the storm and gauging its winds. With such information available, we can prepare for the storm and avoid or evacuate dangerous areas.

In the Christian life, on the other hand, there are no meteorologists. There are no spiritual doppler radar images tracing the roaring lion; there are no spiritual weather updates with full-color images spelling out the spiritual danger in the coming days; there are no airplanes dropping instruments into the swirling clouds to measure wind speed and the scope and size of the hurricane winds; there is no heavenly emergency warning system that interrupts your television program to tell you the storm is coming; there is no angelic speaker system in the sky blaring the news: "Tomorrow trouble is going to land on your doorstep!"

So, what do we do? We walk with God today, always obeying Him, so that we will be right where we need to be tomorrow.

Natural Disasters Reshape Our Value System to Focus on Superior Things

Suffering and trouble tend to empty our hands of things that are earthly and guide us back to things that are godly. They change our focus from comfort to character, from earthly pleasure to the pleasure of God, from wealth to wisdom, and from health to holiness.

The psalmist wrote: "It is good for me that I was afflicted, that I may learn your statutes" (Psalm 119:71). The obvious implication here is that the believer *will* experience affliction—sickness, trial, natural disaster—not *because* he sinned, but to keep him from sinning even more.

This was also the testimony of the apostle Paul:

> Because of the surpassing greatness of the revelations, for this reason, to keep me from exalting myself, there was given me a thorn in the flesh, a messenger of Satan to torment me—to keep me from exalting myself! (2 Corinthians 12:7)

Natural disasters reveal what is most important.

Suffering kept Paul spiritually minded.

At times of natural disasters and calamities in general, we are reminded of what matters most.

Natural Disasters Remind the World of a Coming Disaster and a Final Judgment

No storm we witness can be compared to the storms reserved for the world in the coming tribulation. Following the rapture of the church, the Lord Himself will unleash nature in horrific ways that are unimaginable to mankind.

In his description in Revelation of the final days of human history, John presents a world inundated and impacted by drought, flood, hailstorms, wildfires that consume a third of all the trees, loss of drinking water, famine, disease and rampant epidemics, predatory animal attacks, plagues, mega-earthquakes, and meteorites striking the earth's surface. The natural catastrophes we see today are just a whisper of the coming thunder of God's wrath, a mere shadow compared to the lightning of His holy judgment, which will come upon the earth and everyone who has rejected Jesus Christ as Lord and Savior.

Unbelievers scramble to find an escape clause by denying the existence of a creator God, as Voltaire, the French atheist, did when he wrote that humans are essentially insects living on atoms of mud.[9]

The truth is we will all live forever, experiencing either the justice of the Lord or the joy of the Lord, either facing the full effects of the curse forever or trusting in the Savior who faced the curse and defeated its consequences.

FINAL RESCUE FROM WILD NATURE

In Genesis 2:15-17, God warned Adam that if he chose to disobey his Creator, he would face terrible consequences. After Adam's rebellion, God informed him of some changes brought about by his sin: Adam would *sweat* in his labor. He would try to tame the earth to produce food, but the earth, from that moment on, would resist him by producing an abundance of thistles and *thorns*. Finally, Adam would experience *death*, just as we will eventually (Genesis 3:17-19).

But Jesus, the "last Adam" as Paul called Him (1 Corinthians 15:45; cf. Romans 5:12-21), entered into this cursed and chaotic world. In the garden of Gethsemane, He *sweat*. Indeed, He sweat great drops of blood in the labor of redeeming us from the curse. Then He was crucified, wearing on his brow a crown of *thorns*. Finally, Jesus *died*.

Nature gone wild is both a warning of future judgment and an invitation to believe in Christ, who experienced the effects of a world cursed by sin: sweat, thorns, and death.[10]

Jesus Christ, the Son of God, entered the chaos of a cursed universe so that He could die for us and rise from the dead to secure for us life in Him forever.

So, let every thunderclap remind you of the awesome power of God.

Let every lightning bolt cause you to revere His holy purity.

Let every flood remind you that His justice overflows in judgment.

Let every hurricane remind you of human weakness and Heaven's safety.

Let every crashing wave remind you that He is able to command them to be still.

Let every trial and every heartache remind you of the coming glory of Christ and sweep you up and higher still upon the Rock of Ages.

> *Rock of Ages, cleft for me,*
> *Let me hide myself in Thee;*
> *Let the water and the blood,*
> *From thy wounded side which flowed,*
> *Be of sin, the double cure,*
> *Save from wrath and make me pure.*

> *While I draw this fleeting breath,*
> *When my eyes shall close in death,*
> *When I rise to worlds unknown*
> *And behold Thee on Thy throne,*
> *Rock of Ages, cleft for me,*
> *Let me hide myself in Thee.*[11]

CHAPTER SIX

TRUTHS FROM THE TINIEST OF TEACHERS

I n the eighteenth century, a revival swept through the American colonies. It became known as the Great Awakening. Jonathan Edwards, one of the leading pastors in that awakening, shaped the movement with his powerful writing and preaching.

In his most famous sermon, "Sinners in the Hands of an Angry God," Edwards used the imagery of a spider hanging from its web by a single strand to illustrate an unbelieving soul hanging by a slender thread over the mouth of hell. He urged the unbeliever not to trust that flimsy thread but to run to the mercy of God and trust in Him for salvation.

Even creepy critters can glorify Christ!

The imagery of sinners trusting in spider webs was not a random illustration. Jonathan Edwards had spent many hours studying spiders as they swung from tree branches spinning their webs. He wrote about the amazing art of spider webs and made drawings of different kinds of strands used in webs.[2]

Edwards explored more than spiders, writing extensively on subjects ranging from flying insects to the colors of the rainbow. Nature became to him a classroom where the gospel could be illustrated, the

Christian encouraged, the unbeliever warned, and the glory of the Creator revealed.

One day, after walking around in a nearby pasture, Edwards wrote:

> As I was walking there, and looked up on the sky and clouds, there came into my mind, so sweet a sense of the glorious majesty and grace of God, that I know not how to express. . . . After this [my conversion] . . . the appearance of everything was altered, there seemed to be . . . divine glory in almost everything. God's excellency, his wisdom, his purity and love, seemed to appear . . . in the sun, moon, and stars; in the clouds and blue sky; in the grass, flowers, trees; in the water and all nature . . . [I fixed myself to] see the lightning play, and hear the majestic and awful voice of God's thunder . . . leading me to sweet contemplations of my great and glorious God.[2]

Edwards did more than just look around. He watched, listened, savored, learned, applied, sang, and ultimately worshipped his Creator as he contemplated creation.

To our own detriment, we often make too little of nature and are not the better for it.

SWEET REVELATION FROM BUSY BEES

Could fragile ecosystems have been developed through evolution?

Charles Spurgeon, the great British pastor from the nineteenth century, preached frequently on the subject of the honeybee and the honeycomb. These creatures are among the tiniest teachers God created for us to observe and study.

A sixteen-ounce jar of honey is the result of hard work over the course of the six weeks of the honey-making season. During this period, several thousand bees must fly a combined 100,000 miles gathering nectar from two million flowers just to make one sixteen-ounce jar of honey![3] One author described honey as "a sweet, condensed garden in your mouth."[4]

According to Genesis 1, God created vegetation on the third day of creation. Then two days later, He created the animals that primarily swarm in flight. So, insects in general, locusts, birds, and bees were created on day five.

This means that God ingeniously created the flowers first. And He created them already blooming and colorful to appear attractive to the bees He would create forty-eight hours later. This way, the flowers would be pollinated by the bees and reproduce, and the bees would gain the nectar they would convert to honey and eat.

No doubt Adam and Eve soon learned how honey is made and within a few months realized how good it tastes. Honey is the original organic sweetener.

Scientists now understand that flowering plants and trees all seem to have flower petals designed to draw bees to the nectar at the center of the flower, as if it were painted with a bull's-eye.

This isn't the result of random mutations over millions of years. It's the result of immediate relationships designed by the Creator. Bees and flowers could not have evolved *separately*, even a few seasons or years apart, for they all would have been doomed to die. Flowers and fruit need the bees, and bees need nectar to live.

One former atheist scientist was converted to Christ following his study of the intricate design of the natural world. He especially noted that the honeybee was a powerful example of divine wisdom.

He described how young bees make the wax for the honeycomb, using tiny wax flakes produced by small glands in their abdomens. They chew the flakes into soft, pliable balls, which are then used by other bees to form hexagonal cells. "This truly is the optimal design, for it holds the maximum amount of honey with a minimal amount of wax."[5]

What a coincidence!

When did the bees figure out the hexagon cell structure of the honeycomb? I wonder how many times they tried a circle, a square, or a triangle, only to see the hive collapse, until one of them finally said, "Hey, let's try a hexagon." They got it right the first time by means of the complex genetic code implanted in them by their Creator.

How do bees know they need to fly many miles, back and forth, carrying nectar to the hive, where other bees know to process it and then place the nectar into those hexagonal cells?

How do they know to gather at night at the hive entrance and begin beating their wings—half of the colony on one side fanning air into the hive, and the other half of the colony on the other side fanning the air out of the hive? This organized effort creates a breeze that increases the rate of water evaporation from the nectar, which is necessary for converting nectar to honey.

And just how do they know when it's the perfect time and temperature to cap off each hexagonal cell, now filled with nourishing food for their winter months?

The complex mechanisms in the hive and the perfectly orchestrated work of the bees stagger our minds. This same former atheist wrote:

> It was too much for me! I was confronted with the fact that if our world's creatures were programmed with complex genetic information, and if the information is only ever seen to come from intelligence, then chance processes over millions of years could not possibly account for the origin of the first honey bee . . . For me, the life of the honey bee became a 'sweet revelation.' The honey bee represents the complexity and mystery of our planet, and the genius of our God, who put it there.[6]

The tiny honeybee has much to teach us about our mighty God.

GRITTY TRUTHS FROM WORKING ANTS

While we don't want ants inside our homes, they have powerful lessons to teach our hearts.

There are two animals in Scripture that we're told to take special note of: birds (Matthew 6:26) and ants (Proverbs 6). The ant might seem like an odd choice for teaching humans anything, but Solomon wrote: "Go to the ant, O sluggard, observe her ways and be wise" (Proverbs 6:6).

Meet Professor Ant

Even the lazy person, without the help of a microscope, can easily discern that the ant is persistent, fearless, organized, and hardworking. The sluggard doesn't even have to get out of bed in order to watch the ants carry away his leftover Pop Tart.

Solomon urges careful observation of the ant, "which, having no chief, officer or ruler, prepares her food in the summer and gathers her provision in the harvest" (Proverbs 6:7-8).

It's evident that Solomon spent some time studying the ants. Among other things, he would have noticed their strength. The average ant can lift forty times its weight. If human beings had that level of strength, we would be able to pick up our car and put it in that parking space without having to learn how to parallel park.

The number of ants per colony is startling as well. An ant colony can be the home of as many as four million ants, who travel through elaborate tunnel systems connecting various chambers.

The ants develop and operate an incredibly complex organization with building projects, site management, construction systems, food services, home management systems, and exploration teams designed to find raw materials, as well as food, for survival.

Imagine being able to build and operate a colony whose population is more than that of Delaware, Alaska, Vermont, and Wyoming combined!

These incredibly strong and smart little creatures provide powerful lessons to the careful observer who wants to be wise.

Ants Work without External Pressures, Ordinances, or Incentives

What most amazed Solomon, however, was not that an ant colony is a complex system housing millions of ants. He focused on how extremely organized an ant colony is despite its apparent lack of leaders. Though "having no chief, officer or ruler, [the ant] prepares her food in the summer and gathers her provision in the harvest" (Proverbs 6:7-8).

First, ants have no "chief." The Hebrew word for "chief" can refer to a judge. There are no judges in the ant colony. The reason for this is simple: nothing ever needs to be taken to court. There are no disputes. Imagine Delaware, Alaska, Vermont, and Wyoming shutting down their court systems and releasing all their judges because their services were no longer needed.

Second, ants have no "officer." The Hebrew word here carries the nuance of a civil servant or administrator. The term literally refers to someone who writes something down. His writing may be in a negative or punitive context.

The police officer is an example of someone who writes something down in a punitive or negative manner. If you exceed the speed limit as you drive your car, he might pull you over and write something down . . . it's called a ticket.

Imagine a society of people getting along with millions of other residents and fulfilling their tasks without ever needing a police officer!

Ants evidently get along without a rule book.

Third, ants have no "ruler." The term seems to have the general sense of "one who governs the conduct of a subordinate."[7]

In other words, there are no supervisors in the ant colony. Ants fulfill their tasks and responsibilities without a boss barking orders or, on that rare occasion, delivering a compliment. Ants don't need someone watching over them to make sure they do their work. They perform their tasks and get them done on time. Solomon specifically mentioned that the colony meets its summer and autumn deadlines: She "prepares her food in the summer and gathers her provision in the harvest" (Proverbs 6:8).

The story is told of a man who went to the home in which he had lived twenty years earlier. He asked the owner if he could just walk through his old house. The owner agreed. When he got up into the attic, he found his old jacket. He tried it on and then reached into the pocket. There he found a receipt from a shoe repair shop. Twenty years earlier, he had taken his shoes to the shop and had forgotten to pick them up.

On a whim, and just for fun, he decided to go to the shoe shop. He walked in, handed the man the receipt, and with a straight face asked, "Are my shoes ready?"

Without saying a word, the shoemaker went into the workroom. After a few minutes, he came back to the counter and said, "Come back a week from Thursday."[8]

Ants have a work ethic that challenges the average shoemaker . . . or employee. They work diligently without need of external pressures, ordinances, incentives, or bonuses.

Ants Focus Highly on Communication and Cooperation

In order for ants to accomplish their annual deadlines, they employ staggering communication systems that involve the release of chemical signals into the air. Scientists have discovered dozens of different chemical messages used for communication.

For instance, if a foraging ant decides to veer off the trail previously marked by another ant and blaze a new path, it releases a complex mixture of chemicals to mark the path at the intersection where it veered off. That informs other ants that they are welcome to follow along.

If, however, that same ant finds no food, it tracks back to that same intersection and releases another chemical scent that communicates the message: "This is a dead end." No other ant wastes its time on that path.

On the other hand, if this foraging ant decides to blaze a new trail and finds a caterpillar that's too big to handle, it fires off chemicals into the air that essentially read: "Help!" When other ants arrive, they already know, based on that chemical message released in the air, what tools are needed and how many ants are required to carry the caterpillar back to the colony.[9]

Ants Serve according to Their Divinely Created Design

According to God's creative design, ants fulfill different roles in a given colony. Some are created to serve as worker ants and some as soldier ants or scout ants. And, of course, there is a queen ant. Nobody tries to move up the career ladder.

There are no promotions, and there is no competition. Scout ants are not seeking to overthrow the queen ant, whose primary job is laying thousands of eggs every day. Who would want that job?

God designed each ant to play a role in the same way He designed each believer to play a role in the body of Christ, the church, utilizing his or her spiritual gifts for the edification of the entire church. Peter wrote:

> As each one has received a special gift, employ it in serving one another as good stewards of the manifold grace of God. Whoever speaks, is to do so as one who is speaking the utterances of God; whoever serves is to do so as one who is serving by the strength which God supplies; so that in all things God may be glorified through Jesus Christ, to whom belongs the glory and dominion forever and ever. Amen. (1 Peter 4:10-11)

Peter's focus is not on the gift received but the gift exercised for the benefit of the church. He didn't write, "As each of us has received a special gift, turn it into a trophy, put it on the mantle, and admire it every time you walk by." The point is to use it for the sake of others.

We live in a self-centered culture that can easily invade the church. One news article reported that there are 93 million selfies taken every day and 1,000 selfies posted to Instagram every ten seconds.

People are absorbed in their own lives and enamored with their own reflection.

That would be harmful to any ant colony . . . and to any church family.

Ants Refuse to Give In, Give Up, or Just Get By

The second law of thermodynamics, known as the law of entropy, states that in a closed system disorder always *increases* with time. My college roommate proved that truth nearly every week. Okay, I helped.

All things move toward disorder. One author warned:

> When you become apathetic or complacent or settle for the path of least resistance in some area of life, entropy sets in and dreams die and hopes fade. Then a terrible thing happens: you learn you can live with mediocrity. It's not a great life, but you [learn to] tolerate it.[10]

Sadly, this is true. Instead of pushing forward, we push autopilot. Instead of pursuing excellence, we become satisfied with incompleteness.

The sluggard of Proverbs 6 can include somebody who simply decides to get by. His motto in life is, "Don't sweat the details . . . what's so bad about mediocrity?"

Solomon said, "Go to the ant, O Sluggard. Observe her ways and be wise" (Proverbs 6:6). The same biblical author wrote, "Whatever your hand finds to do, do it with *all* your might" (Ecclesiastes 9:10).

And that's a huge lesson to learn . . . taught by the tiniest of creatures.

CHAPTER SEVEN

THE METAMORPHIC PHENOMENA

In 1937, a man named Frank was diagnosed with hypertension, a health condition barely understood at the time. At the age of fifty-four, his blood pressure was 162/98. This number was considered mild by the medical community of the time.

In 1940, his blood pressure was running 180/88. Still, no treatment was initiated or medical advice offered. By 1941, his pressure had risen to 188/105 and only then his doctors told him to cut back on his work. He tried, but his condition did not improve.

Four years later, Frank's blood pressure was 260/145. On April 12, 1945, he had a severe headache. His blood pressure was 300/190. Later that day, he lost consciousness and died at age sixty-three.

You probably know him better as Franklin Delano Roosevelt, the thirty-second president of the United States.[1]

There were things going on inside his body that he didn't understand, and neither did the medical doctors committed to his care.

As believers, we live in a world that does not understand the *invisible* issues of the heart. The stress and struggles we face inflict damage, not necessarily to blood vessels, but to our spirit and mind.

The good news is that we belong to the Great Physician, who knows exactly what we need. In His inspired manual on the human condition, God sometimes refers to that need in terms of transformation. And the principle of spiritual transformation is not only revealed in Scripture; it's also illustrated physically in the natural world. In nature, this fascinating process of transformation is called *metamor-*

phosis. This term comes from the Greek verb *metamorphoō*, which means "to remodel" or "to change from one form into another."[2]

Metamorphosis, then, might refer to something new and improved by alteration or something entirely new in form and function.

The metamorphic phenomenon takes place in the natural world in a variety of ways and provides a wonderful illustration of changes that are taking place in our own heart and life right now. Even though we might be oblivious to it all, God is at work.

We're going to look at three metamorphic phenomena in nature that occur in three specific environments. They provide powerful lessons for the believer.

THE METAMORPHOSIS OF ROCK INTO GEMSTONE

The first phenomenon is the metamorphosis of certain rocks into gemstones or other rocks of great value. The process takes place because of *the principle of pressure.*

At some point in the past, a given rock beneath the earth's crust underwent intense pressure and heat, causing the atoms to recombine into a new form called metamorphic rock. Through the movement of the earth's crust and the eruption of volcanoes, this rock was carried closer to the surface, where it can be mined.

Marble is an example of metamorphic rock. It forms when limestone is subjected to enough heat and pressure. The calcite in the limestone recrystallizes, and over time with continued pressure, it becomes the marble for your new countertop.

Diamonds are metamorphic rocks made from graphite under great pressure. They are the hardest natural substance found on earth. Even the prophet Jeremiah spoke of an inerasable record written with a pen that had a *diamond* point (Jeremiah 17:1).

Like a disciple developed under pressure

Almost all diamonds are formed one hundred miles or more below the earth's surface. They are carried upward through crustal movements and rising, hot magma. Many were brought up by the eruption of water from beneath the earth's crust during the great flood of Noah's time.

Without that intense pressure miles beneath the earth's surface, graphite remains graphite, and we use it in pencils. But if it undergoes incredible pressure, the metamorphosis produces something so beautiful and stunning that royalty have used it in their crowns and scepters from ancient times.

To this day, diamonds are the most intensely sought gemstone. This is especially true in the Western world over the past seventy years or so, due in large part to a successful advertising campaign launched in 1947 by DeBeers Incorporated. That campaign was called "A Diamond is Forever." Six years later, in a popular film the actress Marilyn Monroe sang "A Diamond Is a Girl's Best Friend."

Thanks to advertising and movie stars, we've been deeply in debt ever since!

It's interesting to consider that though a pencil and a diamond are made of the same substance (carbon), nobody wears a pencil around the neck for jewelry. And no gentleman ever dared to propose by pulling out a pencil and saying, "Sweetheart, did you know that graphite and diamonds are made of the same carbon atoms? Look at the tip on this pencil; it must be the size of a two-carat diamond . . . will you marry me?" Marry him? She would probably use that pencil to cause him a painful death.

Your sweetheart doesn't want a pencil from the grocery store next door. She wants something from a hundred miles below the surface of the planet, something forged from great pressure and heat which represents the strength and beauty of your love.

In Romans 5, the apostle Paul employs the Greek word *thlipsis*, translated "pressure" or "tribulation," in talking about how our walk with Christ becomes that much more valuable, exquisite, and strong. He describes a chain reaction that brings about spiritual transformation in the life of the believer.

And not only this, but we also exult in our tribulations, knowing that tribulation brings about perseverance; and perseverance, proven character; and proven character, hope. (Romans 5:3-4)

God is taking ordinary "graphite" believers and transforming us into diamonds through the pressures we experience—the pressure of deadlines, expectations, finances, relationships, health, job loss, grief, and major life events that bring hardship and difficulty.[3]

Paul teaches that the principle of pressure is a part of God's plan in the metamorphosis of our character, demeanor, perspective, and testimony.

Extreme pressure is extremely productive in producing the character of Christ within us.

THE METAMORPHOSIS OF CERAMIC INTO PORCELAIN

The second phenomenon is the metamorphosis of ceramic into porcelain, a process that occurs only due to *the principle of refinement.*

Technically, porcelain is a form of ceramic. The word *ceramic* refers to clay forms in general and derives from the Greek term *keramos,* which means "potter's clay" or "earthen vessel."

The earliest pottery forms archaeologists have excavated include jars, figurines, and hand-held oil lamps.

It was only in the fourteenth century that European merchants encountered Chinese porcelain, and they were mesmerized by its beauty.

Normal ceramic is thick, porous, grainy, soft, and easily cracked or broken.

A coffee mug is a good example of simple pottery. Beside the fact that it is inexpensive and

How does Christ refine us?

unsophisticated in general, it is porous, which is why it can't keep your drink hot for very long.

Porcelain items, on the other hand, are different. They are referred to at times as *fine china* for a good reason. Many people collect porcelain pieces from different countries they have visited while traveling around the world. They are works of art full of intricate and complex patterns.

But porcelain happens to be pottery. Just like that simple coffee mug, porcelain is made of clay. The primary difference between regular pottery and porcelain is the application of heat. When ordinary pottery is fired at higher temperatures, it can produce a porcelain tile, cup, or saucer that is much smoother, more watertight, and more resistant to staining and chipping.

The key is the heating and cooling process.

The apostle Peter employed the terminology of this process as he encouraged the believer:

> Beloved, do not be surprised at the fiery ordeal among you, which comes upon you for your testing . . . but to the degree that you share the sufferings of Christ, keep on rejoicing . . . if anyone suffers as a Christian, he is not to be ashamed, but is to glorify God in this name. (1 Peter 4:12-13, 16)

This is the principle of refinement—through the fire of trials, the believer is refined. This was the confidence of Job, who wrote: "But He [God] knows the way I take; when He has tried me, I shall come forth as gold" (Job 23:10).

THE METAMORPHOSIS OF CATERPILLAR INTO BUTTERFLY

This is the metamorphic process with which most people are familiar—a caterpillar turns into a butterfly, a completely different creature. This occurs due to *the principle of radical change*.

With the aid of modern DNA analysis and MRIs, scientists are discovering things about this transformation that earlier generations couldn't know, much less watch.

The butterfly goes through four stages in its life cycle: the egg, the larva (caterpillar), the pupa, and the adult butterfly.

Once the egg is hatched, the caterpillar (or larva) emerges. In this short stage, the larva mostly eats a given type of plant. Its mother knew just where to deposit the egg because the caterpillar starts eating as soon as it emerges. In fact, eating is pretty much all the caterpillar does.

By the time the caterpillar finishes growing, it will reach over *three thousand times* its original size. That would be the equivalent of a six-pound baby growing to the size of an elephant in just a few weeks.

When the eating frenzy eventually ends, the caterpillar spins a cocoon, or molts, into a chrysalis (protective covering) and disappears from sight.

With the help of MRIs and other sophisticated equipment, scientists have been able to watch what had been a secret for thousands of years.

In this third stage, known as the pupa, the entire caterpillar actually dissolves all of its tissues in the cocoon into a "caterpillar soup." This liquefied content—groups of cells—now provides the building materials to form the butterfly.

The cells form legs; antennae; a mouth that no longer crunches leaves but sucks nectar; wings that are scale-covered, intricately patterned, and painted with color; a new digestive tract designed for an entirely different appetite; an elaborate vision system through a new set of compound eyes; a complex and new breathing system that powers their flight through the air; and much more.

After breaking free from the cocoon, the adult butterfly sits still for about twenty minutes. During this time, it pumps fluid into its wings, expanding and stretching them as they dry in the air. Then it flaps its glorious wings and without any flight practice, it takes off in the air.[4]

The metamorphosis of a caterpillar into a butterfly beautifully illustrates a powerful spiritual reality.

In his letter to the Roman believers, Paul wrote:

> And do not be conformed to this world, but be transformed [*metamorphoō*] by the renewing of your mind, so that you may prove what the will of God is, that which is good and acceptable and perfect. (Romans 12:2)

Paul's telling believers not to allow themselves to be conformed to the mindset of the world system. And what is that mindset? It's an atheistic, naturalistic worldview which spreads the propaganda that the universe began by an accident, will end by another accident, and we're all here as the result of millions of years of random accidents.

The accidental life is not worth living because it has no meaning, definition, or purpose.[5] This worldview, in the end, leads people to desperation. One celebrity chef and TV personality wore a tattoo on his arm in the Greek language that read, "I am certain of nothing." He ended up taking his own life.

How radically different from the world is the believer who can say with confidence, "I am certain of my Creator and my purpose to live for His glory. I am certain of the gospel—of my Savior and His resurrection. And I am certain of my future, eternal destiny!"

Unfortunately, the worldly mentality, with its amoral and immoral standards for life, has infiltrated the church. Many individuals who claim to be Christians have been conformed to the world's way of thinking.

A recent poll highlighted what has been called the new moral code among people who claim to be practicing Christians—they attend church, pray over their meals, read the Bible, and give money to charity. Below are several statements from the poll and the percentage of Christians who agreed:

- "Any kind of sexual expression between two consenting adults is acceptable"—40%.
- "The highest goal of life is to enjoy it as much as possible"—66%.
- "The best way to find yourself is by looking within yourself"—76%.
- "People should not criticize someone else's life choices"—76%.[6]

It's possible for Christians to be molded by the world instead of being molded by the Word. Keep in mind that Paul is addressing Christians when he commands, "Do not be conformed to this world, but be transformed by the renewing of your mind" (Romans 12:2). The verbs here are present tense, indicating the need for an ongoing, continual refusal to conform to the world and a continual renewal of the mind according to God's Word.

Paul also wrote: "Therefore if anyone is in Christ, he is a new creature; the old things passed away; behold, new things have come" (2 Corinthians 5:17).

Just like the butterfly is a new creature completely different from the caterpillar, so is the believer in Christ.

Just like the butterfly, the believer has a new appetite. The apostle Peter wrote that we should, "like newborn babies, long for the pure milk of the word, so that by it you may grow in respect to salvation" (1 Peter 2:2).

Just like the butterfly, believers have new patterns in life:

> In reference to your former manner of life . . . lay aside the old self, which is being corrupted in accordance with the lusts of deceit . . . be renewed in the spirit of your mind, and put on the new self, which in the likeness of God has been created in righteousness and holiness of the truth. (Ephesians 4:22-24)

In order to mature as a believer, we need all three principles of metamorphosis at work in our lives.

- Pressure helps us to develop perseverance to shine as diamonds for the Lord.

- Refinement helps us to trust our Savior in the flames that purify our character.

- Patterns are changed, along with perspectives, as brand-new creatures in Christ.

CHAPTER EIGHT

BIRD-WATCHING FOR THE WISE

O ne of the most prominent animal species mentioned in Scripture is birds. Birds appear throughout the Bible, creating numerous analogies and applications of biblical truth.

Birds blanket the earth with their presence; they number in the multiplied millions upon millions today. Their vast number highlights the omniscience of God, who says, "I know *every* bird of the mountains" (Psalm 50:11a). Imagine that—there are *billions* of living birds, yet at any given moment, God knows about every one of them.

In the New Testament, Jesus made an even more significant announcement concerning God's care and knowledge of the little birds: "Are not two sparrows sold for a cent? And yet not one of them will fall to the ground apart from your Father" (Matthew 10:29).

This announcement became incredibly encouraging to Joni Eareckson Tada. As a teenager, she broke her neck in a diving accident in the Chesapeake Bay. The tragedy left her totally and permanently paralyzed from the neck down. Twenty-five years later, as she served the Lord full-time, Joni developed some health problems and had to stay in bed. Hoping to cheer her up, her husband, Ken, hung a bird feeder outside her window. At first, it only made her more miserable because she envied the birds' freedom and mobility.

But then she remembered Jesus' words concerning the sparrows.

*More important
than birds*

I glanced at the bird feeder and smiled. I could understand Jesus noticing an eagle . . . But a scrappy sparrow? They're a dime a dozen. Jesus said so himself. Yet from thousands of bird species the Lord chose the most insignificant, least-noticed, scruffiest bird of all. A pint-sized thing that even dedicated birdwatchers ignore. That thought alone calmed my fears. I felt significant and noticed . . . If the great God of heaven concerns himself with a ragtag little sparrow clinging to the bird feeder outside my window, he cares about you.[1]

This happens to be the only animal species Jesus personally commanded us to study. The Lord said, "Look at the birds of the air, that they do not sow, nor reap nor gather into barns, and yet your heavenly Father feeds them" (Matthew 6:26).

Jesus wasn't simply suggesting a casual look. The verb translated "look" (*emblepō*) is an imperative. Jesus was issuing a command, using a word that means to study, consider, or observe the birds.[2]

The German Reformer Martin Luther wrote centuries ago on this text that the Lord "is making the birds our schoolmasters and teachers. It is a great and abiding disgrace to us that in the Gospel a helpless sparrow should become a theologian and a preacher to the wisest of men."[3]

Let's take a closer look at the birds. Pair your binoculars with your Bible, and start studying them. The birds will illustrate theological truths to the wisest Christians among us.

Many know John Stott as a well-respected pastor and theologian, but few are aware that he was an avid bird-watcher. He even coined a term for his lifelong observations of birds. He took the word *ornithology* (the study of birds) and gave it a little twist, originating the term *orni-theology*.

Stott wrote a book titled *The Birds, Our Teachers: Biblical Lessons from a Lifelong Bird-Watcher*. In this book, he stressed, "Many Christians have a good doctrine of redemption, but need a better doctrine of creation. We ought to pursue at least one aspect of natural history."[4]

Like Stott, those who choose to study the birds will discover some important spiritual lessons. We'll look at four of them.

AN EXAMPLE OF PERSISTENCE IN ASSIGNMENTS FROM GOD

Perhaps you're tired today. Life can be redundant and daily tasks demanding. There is always so much to do and so little time!

One author discovered years ago why he was so tired:

> Yes, I'm tired. For several years I've been blaming it on middle age, iron poor blood, lack of vitamins, air pollution, water pollution, saccharin, obesity, dieting . . . and a dozen other maladies that make you wonder if life is really worth living.
>
> But now I find out, tain't that.
>
> I'm tired because I'm overworked.
>
> The population of this country is over 200 million. Eighty-four million are retired. That leaves 116 million to do the work. There are 75 million in school, which leaves 41 million to do the work. Of this total, there are 22 million employed by the federal government.
>
> That leaves 19 million to do the work. Four million are in the armed forces, which leaves 15 million to do the work. Take from that total the 14,800,000 people who work for the state and city governments, and that leaves 200,000 to do the work. There are 188,000 in hospitals, so that leaves 12,000 to do the work. But there are 11,998 people in prisons. That leaves just 2 people to

Perseverence in flight

do the work. You and me. And you're standing there reading this. No wonder I'm tired.[5]

For the weary, one of the most amazing birds to observe is the hummingbird.

Hummingbirds are like miniature helicopters on steroids—able to fly up, down, sideways, backwards, forwards, and even upside down as they loop around and then suddenly come to a standstill, hovering in midair.

The hummingbird's wings beat on average 25 times a second. When they want to show off, their wings beat 80 times a second. And when they are chasing after a potential mate, the wings can beat 200 times a second, the same rate as that of a housefly.[6]

In his book about hummingbirds, Crawford Greenewalt wrote that hummingbirds have the highest energy output per unit of weight of any living warm-blooded animal. The average person's output of calories is around 3,500 calories a day. The equivalent for the hummingbird is 155,000 calories a day! A normal person eats 2.5 pounds of food daily (with the exception of Thanksgiving!), and if our output of daily energy matched that of a hummingbird, we would have to eat *370 pounds* of food a day. That's a lot of cheesecake.

Hummingbirds are constantly eating, consuming what amounts to half their weight in sugar every single day.[7]

Hummingbirds hardly ever stop moving. They're a great example of Solomon's divine counsel: "Whatever your hand finds to do, do it with all your might" (Ecclesiastes 9:10).

The apostle Paul also provides encouragement with regard to the most redundant, repetitive, challenging, and difficult chores of life. He considers all of it nothing less than an act of worship, writing, "Whether, then, you eat or drink or whatever you do, do all to the glory of God" (1 Corinthians 10:31).

Watch the persistent activity of a hummingbird for a few minutes; then get up and tackle the next thing on your list as an offering of worship to your creator God.

A PICTURE OF THE PROTECTING CARE OF GOD

Birds appear rather frequently in the Bible as a symbol of God's protection over His own people.

In the great song of Moses recorded in Deuteronomy 32, the Lord is compared to an eagle that stirs up its nest and hovers over its young, spreading its wings over them for protection (verse 11).

Isaiah the prophet addressed a nation fearful of their future, proclaiming that God was hovering over the Israelites as birds hover in the sky watching all that takes place below (Isaiah 31:5).

The protective nature of birds becomes an illustration of our creator God.

Bluebirds swoop down on squirrels to keep them from getting too close to their nest. Verbal battles occur in the skies as crows chase away hawks from their young.

The eider duck sits on her ducklings, shielding them in the open without any natural cover. She is so dedicated to protecting her young that she sits still even when intruders lurk around. In fact, she will sit tight until an intruder actually touches her. She is literally *a sitting duck*—lacking protection for herself while shielding her young from predators, from the heat of the tropical sun, or from the bitter cold of an Arctic blizzard.[8]

Several times in the Psalms, David alludes to a bird's care for its young as an illustration of God's much greater care for His own. He writes to the Lord in Psalm 61:4, "Let me take refuge in the shelter of Your wings." With a sense of determination, he writes in yet another psalm, "My soul takes refuge in You; and in the shadow of Your wings I will take refuge" (Psalm 57:1).

In essence, David is saying, "Lord, you are available and faithful, and I will place myself in your care."

At one point, when David is desperate and in peril in the wilderness of Judah, he writes, "For you have been my help, and in the shadow of your wings I sing for joy" (Psalm 63:7).

When the widow Naomi returned to Bethlehem with her recently widowed daughter-in-law, Ruth, there was little hope for either of them. They would have food only if they could find a godly farmer who was still obeying the law, leaving the grain in the corners of his fields for the poor and allowing them to glean the leftover grain after the reapers had passed through (Leviticus 19:9-10). They were living during the days of the Judges, however, when "everyone did what was right in his own eyes" (Judges 21:25). It was everyone for himself!

But there was an older, godly farmer named Boaz who was still obeying the Word of the Lord. The poor, and widows were almost always poor, were allowed to glean in his fields of grain. Ruth ended up getting a sizable amount of grain, and Farmer Boaz ended up getting a wife.

When Boaz first met Ruth in the field, he said to her, "May the Lord reward your work, and your wages be full from the Lord, the God of Israel, under whose wings you have come to seek refuge" (Ruth 2:11-12).

In the next chapter, Ruth uses the same imagery when she sneaks out to the threshing floor to essentially propose to Boaz. She says to him, "Spread your covering over your maid" (Ruth 3:9). The Hebrew word translated "covering" is the same word Boaz used months earlier in Ruth 2:12, where it is translated "*wings.*"

Ruth is essentially saying, "I'm glad you have been praying that God would cover me with His wings, but I'm convinced He wants *you* to take care of that responsibility!" Boaz gladly agrees.

Birds provide a wonderful picture of God's care and protection of His people.

AN ILLUSTRATION OF THE MYSTERIOUS WAYS OF GOD

In the book of Job, God uses a bird to illustrate His mysterious ways.

When God finally comes to Job to redeem him from the pit of despair, instead of answering Job's questions, He takes Job on a tour of creation. God shows him, among other things, one particular bird we probably would have skipped over in the tour—the ostrich. God explains:

> The ostriches' wings flap joyously with the pinion and plumage of love, for she abandons her eggs to the earth and warms them in the dust, and she forgets that a foot may crush them, or that a wild beast may trample them. She treats her young cruelly, as if they were not hers; though her labor be in vain, she is unconcerned; because God has made her forget wisdom, and has not given her a share of understanding. (Job 39:13-17)

God designs strange creatures

The ostrich is not the brightest bird on the planet, and it is quite odd in many respects. Growing as tall as nine feet and weighing around four hundred pounds, the ostrich is the largest bird in the world today. Though it has wings, it cannot fly. Since the ostrich can't fly up to the top of a tree or cliff, the female lays her eggs in a hole dug in the sand.

God mentions here that the ostrich forgets where she lays her eggs, or at least she appears unconcerned, probably due to somewhat limited intelligence.

Pliny, the first-century Roman naturalist, wrote that the ostrich hides its head in the bushes when a dangerous predator is nearby, assuming it is hidden and safe because it cannot see the predator.[9] But for all its strange ways, lack of memory, and downright ignorance, the ostrich is amazing to watch as it runs: "When she lifts herself on high, she laughs at the horse and his rider" (Job 39:18).

Lifting her head and extending her small wings for balance, she takes off running. Horses can gallop at forty miles per hour at top speed, while ostriches can reach a speed of fifty miles per hour.[10]

Xenophon, the Greek general and historian who lived four hundred years before the birth of Christ, once wrote that some of his soldiers hunted the bird but no one succeeded in catching it. The "horsemen who hunted the bird soon desisted from the pursuit; for it far outstripped them in its flight, using its feet for running, and its wings, raising them like a sail."[11] At top speed, the ostrich's footsteps are twenty feet apart.[12]

Job endured incredible suffering. He lost all his children, his businesses, workers, cattle, camels, and health. And he lost everything in freak accidents or unexpected raids by cruel invaders. Did he really want to listen to God describe an ostrich when it runs?

This was God's way of telling Job that He creates things we would never think of creating; He designs creatures and natural wonders that we would never design, especially when they seem to make no sense at all.

Perhaps you've been confronted with situations that cause you to ask, "Lord, what in the world are You doing? What were You thinking when You allowed that? Lord, what have You created in my world? It makes about as much sense as a huge bird that can't fly but runs faster than a horse."

Some of God's purposes, designs, and ways have to go under the categorical heading of "Unexpected," "Impossible to Understand," or "Without an Explanation from God" (see Isaiah 55:8-9).

Perhaps God created the ostrich to provide an illustration of His mysterious ways, a reminder that His ways and thoughts are much higher than ours.

A PATTERN OF RETURNING TO WALK WITH GOD

In his book, John Stott has an entire chapter entitled "Repentance." On the first page is a photograph he had taken of a white stork on top of her nest.

At this point, you're probably thinking, as I did, that Stott is going a little too far with the analogies. Birds don't repent since animals do not willfully violate the law of God and sin. They're never overwhelmed with guilt about stealing another animal's food; they never feel guilty over biting people or not sharing their food with homeless animals.

So what do birds have to do with *repentance*?

Stott cites a text from Jeremiah that makes a direct analogy between the migration of birds and the disobedient and unrepentant people of Judah:

> I have listened and heard, they have spoken what is not right; no man repented of his wickedness, saying, "What have I done?" Everyone turned to his course, like a horse charging into the battle. Even the stork in the sky knows her seasons; and the turtledove and the swift and the thrush observe the time of their migration; but My people do not know the ordinance of the LORD. (Jeremiah 8:6-7)

Jeremiah was aware, as we are today, that the land of Israel is a corridor of bird migration. It is a highway for birds called a *flyway*.

Many species fly south in the fall through the Strait of Istanbul, a waterway that forms a boundary between Europe and Asia. They travel across Turkey and then down through Israel into the warmer climates of Africa. Without fail, when spring arrives, they all return through Israel and then fan out into Europe and Asia.[13]

Bird migration = repentance

Perhaps Jeremiah singled out storks because he had watched their huge flocks winging southward. It is estimated that nearly 500,000 storks migrate over the Middle East every spring and fall.

Speaking through Jeremiah, God rebuked His people for being *unlike* the storks who had the sense to know when they needed to come home.

What birds do by instinctive navigational skills (something scientists are unable to understand), God's people should do regularly. Whenever we leave the flyway—the right path—we should repent and return to our forgiving Creator. "Would that we had as strong a homing instinct *spiritually* as birds have *physically*!"[14]

Let's not postpone our flight back home to the Savior.

THE WONDER OF YOU

Augustine (AD 354–430), the brilliant philosopher and theologian who served as the bishop of Hippo (North Africa), wrote in his famous work Confessions:

> Here are men going afar to marvel at the heights of mountains, the mighty waves of the sea, the long courses of great rivers, the vastness of the ocean, the movements of the stars, yet leaving themselves unnoticed and not seeing it as marvelous.[1]

While observing many elements of the natural world, it's easy to neglect the marvelous aspects of *our* creation by God.

Consider the brain. In this command center, there are 100 billion neurons, each one communicating through tens of thousands of connections every single *second*.

The eye is an amazingly complex, self-cleaning, self-adjusting optic marvel. The eye is such an intricate organism that Darwin himself confessed to a friend that his theory had as one of its weakest points the concept of the evolution of the human eye.[2] He wrote later in his life: "The eye to this day gives me a cold shudder, but . . . my reason tells me I ought to conquer this cold shudder."[3]

How tragic that Darwin dismissed that cold shudder. Frankly, the marvels of God's creation become even more evident the deeper we dive into the molecular, cellular structure of our bodies.

THE CELL: THE WONDER OF COMPLEXITY

Naturalism holds that life is an accident that progressively developed over millions of years. Everything started in a warm little pond of goop, where the first amino acids formed millions of years after the big bang. Millions of years later, some of those amino acids made the right connections and eventually, after more millions of years, the first cell sprang to life.

Mankind owes it all to that amazing little puddle of goop!

As the late evolutionist Bertrand Russell put it, man is "a curious accident in a backwater."[4] University of Oxford professor Peter Atkins wrote with even more biting pessimism, "We're just a bit of slime on a planet belonging to one sun."[5]

To the eyes of Darwin, who used the light microscope to study microscopic organisms, the cell indeed looked like a disordered blob of particles that seemed to be tossing around haphazardly in all directions.

Much has changed in science since then, however. The invention of the electron microscope, the amazing progress in molecular biology, and research on mitochondrial DNA have allowed scientists to study a single cell magnified a billion times.

One thing they have learned is that the human body is an amazing cell factory. It produces two million cells every single second, or sixty billion in one day! The total number of cells in the body is thirty-seven trillion.

This production of new cells is a good thing since around two million cells die every second. As the body ages, the replacement rate slows down. This explains some of the problems the body encounters, such as dry skin, weak memory, degenerating eyesight, pain in the joints, and so on.

As staggering as these numbers are, scientists have also discovered that 100 trillion atoms are working inside *every individual cell* in the human body. And these trillions of atoms are *not* tossing around haphazardly.

Despite the absurd claims of naturalists, the discoveries and observations of science point to the hand of a creative, imaginative, brilliant, and purposeful God.

In his book *Evolution: A Theory in Crisis*, Michael Denton attempts to describe the amazing complexity of what takes place inside one cell:

> To grasp the reality of life as it has been revealed by molecular biology, we must magnify a cell a thousand million times until it . . . resembles a giant airship large enough to cover a great city like London or New York.

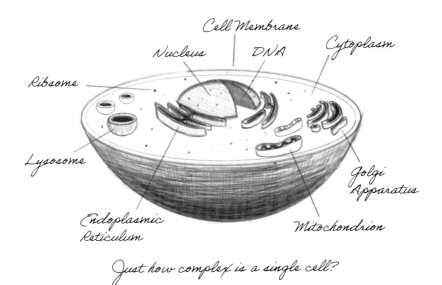

Just how complex is a single cell?

. . . On the surface of the cell, we would see millions of openings, like the port holes of a vast space ship, opening and closing to allow a continual stream of materials to flow in and out. If we were to enter one of these openings...we would see endless highly organized corridors and conduits branching in every direction away from the perimeter of the cell, some leading to the central memory bank in the nucleus and others to assembly plants and processing units. The nucleus itself would be a vast spherical chamber . . . resembling a geodesic dome inside of which we would see, all neatly stacked together in ordered arrays, the miles of coiled chains of the DNA molecules. . . . We would see all around us, in every direction we looked, all sorts of robot-like machines. We would notice that the simplest of the functional components of the cell, the protein molecules, were astonishingly, complex pieces of molecular machinery, each one consisting of about three thousand atoms arranged in highly organized 3-D spatial conformation. We would wonder even more as we watched the strangely purposeful activities of these weird molecular machines, particularly when we realized that, despite all our accumulated knowledge of physics and chemistry, the task of designing one such molecular machine— that is one single functional protein molecule—would be completely beyond our capacity at present and will probably not be achieved until at least the beginning of the next century.[6]

The cell is a wonder of complexity that points to a wonderful Creator.

THE DNA: THE WONDER OF INFORMATION

How does DNA point to a Creator?

Though the cell is complex, its complexity falls short of the extremely intricate details present in DNA. DNA is a molecular structure present in the cells that carries hereditary material passed on from one generation to the next with organized information about growth, development, and reproduction. DNA contains the genetic information for the transmission of inherited traits.[7]

Though DNA was discovered in the late nineteenth century, its role in genetic inheritance was understood only in the mid-twentieth century. Since then, genetic research has advanced tremendously. Besides decoding the human genome in 2003 (a project that started in 1990), scientists have made inroads into the field of epigenetics, which analyzes the genes in greater depth, giving insight into various diseases and conditions and how they can be treated effectively. The potential is enormous.[8]

DNA is formed by approximately three billion base pairs. These are complementary molecules that are bound together to form a "rung" of the DNA "ladder." The base pairs form the building blocks for the double helix design. Within such bases, there are about twenty thousand genes that provide the information on what kind of proteins should be produced. The proteins directly affect the biology of a given individual.[9]

There is so much genetic material in the DNA that if all the DNA inside all of our cells were to be uncoiled and stretched out, it would be twice the diameter of the solar system.[10] All that complexity and design is what makes the marvel of you and me.

The wonder of the DNA goes beyond organized information.

Studies have shown the incredible *beauty* of the DNA. Base pairs of DNA resemble stained-glass windows of intricate and beautiful designs.

When we look at a stained-glass window, we automatically say something like, "Wow! Look at the repeating patterns and the balance of color. That's a beautiful design!" We never say or even think that the window is the result of random pieces of glass lying in a puddle of goop for millions of years until they decided to attach themselves to each other so that by chance they formed amazingly complex and beautiful patterns.

It's an amazing *design*. Somebody had to conceive of that pattern, create the materials, and then arrange them together.

Still, evolutionists maintain that given enough time, atoms could form together to create such design, beauty, functionality, and complexity of information. Just give it enough time!

As many have argued, that would be like expecting a monkey sitting at a keyboard and randomly hitting keys for millions of years to eventually produce a telephone book with each phone number in the numerically correct order and each address spelled correctly.

Neither chance nor time can produce DNA. Only an intelligent Mind can. However, even when *science* hints at the truth of creation, *scientists* dig in their heels in resistance.

Two scientists, Mark Stoeckle at Rockefeller University and David Thaler at the University of Basel, made an astonishing discovery: "All humans alive today are the offspring of a common mother and father." Based on the investigation of DNA "bar codes" of 5 million animals from 100,000 different species, they also concluded that 90 percent of all animal species alive today "sprang into being *recently* from some seminal, Big Bang-like event." Moreover, "all animal species alive today come from parents that all began giving birth at roughly *the same time*, less than a quarter-million years ago." Thaler confessed, "This conclusion is very surprising, and I *fought against* it as hard as I could."[11]

Why would Thaler fight against the conclusion he drew based on DNA evidence? Because of his unquestioning commitment to the naturalistic worldview and the fact that his research was pulling him toward the truth of Genesis 1.

FROM COMPLEXITY TO COMFORT

The complexity seen in the human body leads to one conclusion: we were *created*. And if our creator God is wise and powerful enough to create us, He is wise and powerful enough to *care* for us.

> "Thus says the LORD who made you and formed you from the womb, who will help you, 'Do not fear.'" (Isaiah 44:2)

You are *not* an accident; you are the work of the Master Creator. You were *not* an afterthought; you are the result of eternal thought.

You were deliberately, specifically, and intentionally embroidered by the Master Designer. Consequently, you have no reason to be afraid of your past, present, or future. Everything about your life fits within God's sovereign purpose, even though we might not have all the answers or explanations this side of heaven.

The story is told that in the early 1930s, a man stood on the side of a dirt road next to his broken-down car. He had exhausted himself under the hood of his Model A; nothing he tried would get it to crank back up again.

A beautiful, chauffeur-driven car pulled off the road near him and a small, well-dressed older gentleman got out, walked over, and asked the man if he could take a look under the hood. After a few minutes, he popped his head out from underneath the hood, slammed it shut, and told the man the car could now be started.

It cranked right up.

Unable to contain his curiosity, the man blurted out, "You're not dressed much like a mechanic. How did you know how to fix my car?"

The man quietly responded, "Well, my name is Henry Ford. I *invented* your car, so I know how it's supposed to work."

God designed you. He put you together. He wrote out the design of your life and coded those instructions into the DNA tucked inside the cells of your body. Don't ever underestimate God's creation. You are a uniquely crafted and created masterpiece.

God invented you . . . He knows how you are supposed to work.

This glorious truth should ultimately lead us to humble ourselves before Him and join the psalmist David in saying, "On the glorious splendor of Your majesty and on Your wonderful *works*, I will meditate" (Psalm 145:5).

This is the marvelous truth about *you*.

CHAPTER TEN

THE DAY YOU FINALLY BECOME PERFECT

I f we could travel back in time to the six days of creation, we would be awestruck at the creative genius of our creator God. If we could see Adam and Eve on the sixth day of creation, we would be breathless. They were perfectly formed, sinless in character, unblemished physical specimens, healthy, and strong.

If Adam and Eve could see *us*, they would be speechless as well, filled with grief and pity for what has happened as a result of their original sin. They would be deeply saddened that our health and beauty have been so marred by the effects of sin over thousands of years.[1]

Because of sin, paradise was lost, and sin has run its course for centuries through our own willing submission to the tempter as sons and daughters of Adam and Eve.

But the Creator did not abandon His creation. He promised a Redeemer to bring paradise back. Because of Christ, the last Adam (1 Corinthians 15:45), and His sacrifice for sin and sinners, Satan's ultimate plans were crushed, and paradise will indeed be regained—and so much more!

One of the most remarkable aspects of God's new creation—the new heavens and new earth where we will live forever—will be the radical change to our bodies. As promised, we will resemble not just Adam and Eve, but also our glorified Lord.

Many questions surround this topic. Thankfully, the Lord has given us answers through the apostles. Based on their insights, let's take a closer look at our future, glorified body.

WILL I HAVE A PHYSICAL BODY IN HEAVEN?

The short answer to this question is *yes*, but it will be different. Paul briefly mentioned the transformation of the body in his letter to the Philippians:

> For our citizenship is in heaven, from which also we eagerly wait for a Savior, the Lord Jesus Christ; who will transform the body of our humble state into conformity with the body of His glory, by the exertion of the power that He has even to subject all things to Himself. (Philippians 3:20-21)

Clearly, there's a continuity between the earthly body and the eternal body. You will not die as Fred Smith and live in heaven as Sam Jones. The resurrected, eternal body is the same body you had on earth, but it will be perfected and made eternal like the body of Jesus. Having risen from the dead, our Lord became our prototype. Jesus was still Jesus *after* He arose; He had the same body, but it was different, better, and adapted for a new sphere of existence.

Based on John 20, one significant difference between our glorified bodies and the resurrection body of Jesus is that all our scars will be gone. Jesus, however, chose to retain some of the scars of His crucifixion. In the upper room, He instructed Thomas to touch the nail prints in His hands and His side, where a soldier had pierced Him with a spear (John 20:27).

The scars Jesus retained will serve throughout eternity as an everlasting testimony and tribute to His atoning sacrifice and redemption through His blood for our salvation.

But what, exactly, did Jesus' body *look like* after He rose from the dead?

He looked like a human being. He didn't rise as some alien creature or ghost. He was recognizable to His disciples and spent time eating and talking with His friends (Luke 24:41-43; Acts 10:41). He wasn't a disembodied spirit floating around the room. He had a real, physical, functional, genuinely human body.

But while the resurrected body of Jesus was human, it displayed *superhuman* abilities. He was able to pass through closed walls and doors (John 20:19), appearing and disappearing suddenly (Luke 24:30-31, 36).[2] How exciting to know that we will have glorified bodies that follow the pattern of Jesus' body, experiencing freedom of movement and perfection in every aspect.

WILL MY IMMORTAL BODY FUNCTION LIKE IT DOES NOW?

While our resurrection bodies will exhibit certain superhuman abilities, in a general sense they will function like they do now.

We will inherit a new earth, where the Father's house of gold and glory will rest (Revelation 21–22). Heaven will include a river flowing between orchards of trees. We will see that beautiful place with our *eyes*, smell the flowers and budding trees with our *noses*, taste fruit and enjoy feasting with *mouths and taste buds*, and hear the rushing, cascading river and all the sounds of a new creation with our *ears*. We will fill our *lungs* with air and then with our *voices* join the hosts of heaven in singing praises to our glorious, majestic, creator God.

Scripture describes the new heavens and new earth as places where there will be animals, fruit trees, rivers, feasting, rejoicing, and worshipping. These are literal glimpses into our future, not metaphorical make-believe for the wishful.

We won't be ethereal spirits floating around on heavenly clouds, playing harps all day. There is no theological, grammatical, or contextual reason to spiritualize, doubt, or deny any of these biblical descriptions of our future existence.

According to descriptions in our Lord's preaching, as well as the tour of heaven given to the apostle John, resurrected believers will be capable of watching, talking, walking, kneeling, singing, leaping, listening, eating, touching, and laughing.

In fact, eternity starts with a banquet. Isaiah records that the Lord Himself will make sure the food served at the banquet feast is nothing but the finest of foods: "The LORD of hosts will prepare a lavish banquet for all peoples on this mountain; a banquet of aged wine, choice pieces [of meat] with marrow" (Isaiah 25:6).

WHAT WILL MY IDENTITY BE IN HEAVEN?

The answer to this question is very clear: You will still be you. Your eternal identity will be a continuation of—but perfection of—your identity now. We know this because people in heaven are called by the same name they had on earth. Abraham is still Abraham, Isaac is still Isaac, and Jacob is still Jacob (Matthew 8:11).

The Lord will give us a new name (Revelation 2:17), a reference to unique intimacy we will enjoy with God; our relationship with the Lord will be personal as well as corporate. Our new name does not require the loss of personal and individual identity.[3] We will not reincarnate into some other life-form as Hinduism teaches; neither will we melt into some universal consciousness without any personal identity as Buddhism believes.

In his tour of heaven, the apostle John saw the city of gold surrounded by a wall: "It had a great and high wall, with twelve gates, and at the gates twelve angels; and names were written on them, which are the names of the twelve tribes of the sons of Israel" (Revelation 21:12). In other words, this will be a city of history; Israel's ancient past will not be forgotten.

John saw further: "And the wall of the city had twelve foundation stones, and on them were the twelve names of the twelve apostles of the Lamb" (Revelation 21:14). So, the history of the apostolic era likewise will be remembered.

Judah and Joseph will still be Judah and Joseph; Peter will still be known as Peter, Andrew will still be Andrew; Fred, Susie, John, and Jill will still be Fred, Susie, John, and Jill.

We will continue to be ourselves—but without all the broken-down parts.

WILL MY BODY BE PERFECT IN HEAVEN?

Yes! At last, you will experience physical perfection!

Paul described this to the Corinthians by explaining that in our resurrected bodies, that which is corruptible will be replaced by that which is incorruptible (1 Corinthians 15:42-49). Nothing diseased, dying, deformed, disabling, digressing, or discouraging will ever again be a part of our physical body and emotional state.

There *will* be continuity between our immortal body and the body we now have. We will be recognizable as the same people we are today.

Jesus did not rise from the grave as a fair-skinned, tall, blonde-haired man. He was resurrected as who He was—a Jewish man, which most likely means His skin was bronze and His eyes were brown or black, as was His hair.

If you have blue eyes now, you will have blue eyes in heaven. If you had blonde hair or black hair before it all turned grey, you will go back to the vitality of your youth and have blonde hair or black hair again. For those of us who used to have hair, we're going to get it back!

According to the Bible, we each will be transformed into an immortal specimen of eternal youth and health. We will never again catch a glimpse of ourselves in the mirror and notice wrinkles or blemishes; we will never experience another moment of sickness, injury, or allergy.[4] As Paul described, "This perishable must put on the imperishable, and this mortal must put on immortality" (1 Corinthians 15:53).

Everything mortal will be replaced with immortality; everything that is perishable—that ages, wears out, and doesn't work anymore or never did work correctly—will be removed, and our new body will be imperishable. We will be forever absolute, imperishable *perfection.*

For those in the body of Christ who suffer the greatest imperfections, heaven will only be that much sweeter.

In his book *Heaven*, Randy Alcorn quotes Joni Eareckson Tada, who has been a quadriplegic since her youth:

> I can still hardly believe it. I, with shriveled, bent fingers, atrophied muscles, gnarled knees, and no feeling from the shoulders down, will one day have a new body, light, bright, and clothed in righteousness—powerful and dazzling. Can you imagine the hope this gives someone spinal-cord injured like me? Or someone who is cerebral palsied, brain-injured, or who has multiple sclerosis? Imagine the hope this gives someone who is manic-depressive. No other religion promises new bodies, hearts, and minds. Only in the Gospel of Christ do hurting people find such incredible hope.[5]

Alcorn comments:

> Joni tells of speaking to a class of mentally handicapped Christians. They thought it was great when she said she was going to have a new body. But then she added, "And *you're* going to get new *minds*." The class broke out in cheers and applause. They knew just what they wanted—new minds.[6]

Let me quickly add that our new appearance will be much more magnificent than just a healthy body and a full head of hair.

In one of Jesus' many sermons, He quoted a promise recorded in the book of Daniel: "Then THE RIGHTEOUS WILL SHINE FORTH AS THE SUN in the kingdom of their Father" (Matthew 13:43; see Daniel 12:3).

John described Jesus in His glorified body shining like the sun in its strength (Revelation 1:16). In the event known as the transfiguration, Jesus met with Moses and Elijah on the mountain, and His glory peeked through the veil of flesh for a few moments in time. Peter and the other disciples awoke just in time to see this brilliant display of glory. Luke later described this event in his Gospel, where Jesus, Elijah, and Moses were seen in gleaming, shining brilliance (Luke 9:29-31).

In Exodus 34, Moses went into the presence of the glory of God to receive the tablets of the law. When Moses came down from the mountain, "the skin of his face shone because of his speaking with Him" (verse 29).

There's no reason in Scripture why we can't understand the idea of our glorified bodies shining with brilliant light as a literal fact. God Himself is gloriously bright and brilliant, and as His image-bearers, we will one day be perfected and reflect in our own bodies—in our faces and our own unique manner—the glorious splendor of our Lord. Like Moses on the mountain, our faces—our entire beings—will glow with light.

You won't just have a new body; you will shine with brilliant light throughout the kingdom and into the glories of heaven. Each believer will one day become a *shining immortal*, breathtakingly stunning in splendor, though still unique individually.

WHAT WILL HEAVENLY LIFE BE LIKE IN MY NEW BODY?

One way Satan seeks to discourage believers is by robbing them of all the color, excitement, and breathtaking aspects of heaven. He prefers that we think of heaven as a boring place of continual rest and inactivity. In fact, heaven will be a very active place where our knowledge, skills, abilities, and interests will all be enhanced by our perfected bodies and minds.

The apostle Paul taught that our glorified bodies will be transformed into conformity with Jesus' resurrection body. This suggests that like Jesus we will even be able to materialize and then disappear.

This does not mean we will become divine; just because our bodies will mirror the glory of Christ's glorified body does not mean we will be omnipotent, omnipresent, or omniscient. We will have limitations and the need to learn, and we will have the desire to learn like never before.

Interestingly, while we apparently will have special abilities when it comes to transportation, such abilities may not be commonly employed. The Celestial City is marked by streets of gold, gates, and foundations, which suggest conventional means of transportation. Wheels, motors, automobiles, technology, invention, and artistry certainly are not sinful, so we should not be surprised by the presence of such things in eternity.[7]

The description of the millennial kingdom and even into the eternal state implies culture, development, artistry, music, composition, invention, and technology. Heaven will be a place of incredible creativity. Imagine the music musicians will compose. Imagine the paintings artists will paint! Imagine the new technological inventions and advancements that can be produced by redeemed, immortalized, perfected engineers, working with unclouded and unhindered inventive minds, in full and joyful cooperation with each other.

In the eternal state I believe the Lord will allow and encourage you to use the skills you've developed and the talents He Himself coded into your DNA. You will find freedom, joy, and true worship in continuing to invent, build, paint, compose, discover, and explore the new heavens and earth. Based on the record of Scripture, there is no reason to doubt that these activities will take place *forever* on the new earth and throughout the new universe, given for our eternal enjoyment.

Heaven is not some boring place where you will be all dressed up with nowhere to go. God created you, and one day He will perfect and release you to do everything He creatively built into you for your enjoyment and His glory.

In Psalm 16:11 David described the joy and eternal pleasures of being in the Lord's presence. In heaven we will know the joy of our Lord's presence—of seeing Him and personally thanking Him for His redemption and His grace. We will delight in discovering a world re-created by Him for us to explore and enjoy. This will be a return to a far better garden of Eden. Without sin, we will be able to explore mighty rivers, climb the highest mountains, and even venture into space as new technologies are created to explore the universe.

Pastor Ray Stedman wrote many years ago about the new creation: "There will be new planets to develop, new principles to discover, new joys to experience. Every moment of eternity will be an adventure of discovery."[8]

One of the Lord's promises is that one day our new world will ring with music, joy, conversation, food, nature, and laughter. What happens when friends gather around a table with some good food and conversation? There is laughter.

The Bible often portrays our future as a time of gathering and eating at a dinner table with the Lord. And what sounds will we hear? Laughter.

Jesus promised that in the kingdom to come mourning and grieving will be turned into laughter. "Blessed are you who weep now, for you shall laugh" (Luke 6:21), He said, and, "Be glad in that day and leap for joy, for behold, your reward is great in heaven" (Luke 6:23).

Nobody leaps for joy in silence! We will be shouting, smiling, singing, and laughing for joy.

Heaven will be ringing with laughter. Do you know why? Because "He who began a good work in you will perfect it" (Philippians 1:6).

When we see Him . . . we will *finally* be perfect!

CHAPTER ELEVEN

LIVING THE DREAM

Believers in general entertain a certain degree of curiosity about the life to come and often wish God had revealed more details about heaven and our life for all eternity.

Information on this topic, however, has been divinely limited and reserved. The apostle Paul was given a tour of heaven, where he heard inexpressible words he was not permitted to repeat (2 Corinthians 12:4). Similarly, at one point while John was recording his vision of heaven and things to come in the book of Revelation, he saw an incredibly extensive display of future events. He was preparing to write it down but was commanded to seal the book up and not write those things (Revelation 10:4).

It's as if the Lord essentially says to the Bible student, "I know you want more, but I decided long ago not to give you everything you *want* to know. Instead I've given you everything you *need* to know."

We have received enough information to know we haven't seen anything yet! This world around us, as beautiful and colorful as it is, is a mere shadow of the *living color* to come. Even our bodies, as we saw in the previous chapter, will one day shine with the brilliance of the sun.

Now let's consider some more questions about the life to come. While some of these questions relate to our glorified bodies, others probe into different aspects of life in the new world.

WILL I HAVE EMOTIONS AND FEELINGS?

Yes, we will experience emotions and feelings in heaven.

The Lord has promised that we will leap for joy in that day (Luke 6:23). Frankly, I'm too old to leap. This promise, then, means I'll have not only great emotion but also a return to youthful strength and vitality that will allow me to jump up and down.

God also promised that mourning will turn into laughter (Luke 6:21). In this new world, sad tears will be banned forever; laughing for joy will be established for all eternity. God's servants will be invited to share in their Master's happiness (Matthew 25:23).

One of the misconceptions about heaven is that we will become stoics with no feelings, no laughter, and no tears. The promise of Revelation 21:4—which says our tears will be wiped away—is commonly misinterpreted. In the biblical context, those tears relate to death, separation, and pain.

There are times when we cry for joy upon seeing a beautiful sunset or hearing a beautiful piece of music. God crafted us with unique emotions. Our responses to reunions, relationships, music, a beautiful sunset, stunning scenery, and even a funny story are all going to elicit from us feelings and emotional responses.

We will live the dream! Eternal life with Christ and the redeemed will be so wonderful that we will often cry tears of *joy*.

WILL I ENJOY FRIENDSHIPS AND FAMILY IN HEAVEN?

The answer is *yes*.

Some people have misinterpreted passages like Psalm 73:25, where Asaph wrote: "Whom have I in heaven but you? And besides You, I desire nothing on earth." They conclude we will have no relationships in heaven besides that with God.

However, if we compare Scripture with Scripture and go back to the original creation, we find the triune God saying, "Let Us make man in Our image, according to Our likeness" (Genesis 1:26). The triune God enjoys fellowship among the three Persons—God the Father, God the Son, and God the Spirit. God has always enjoyed divine fellowship.

It's interesting to note that the first time God said something about creation was *not* good, it involved a relationship. Adam had no other human being with whom to converse and share life. God said, "It is *not good* for the man to be *alone*" (Genesis 2:18).

This is fascinating because Adam wasn't alone—he had God! Still, God stated that Adam was, in a unique way, alone.

God designed human beings to have fellowship, community, companionship, and friendship. His greatest commandments, Jesus declared, are to "LOVE THE LORD YOUR GOD WITH ALL YOUR HEART, AND WITH ALL YOUR SOUL, AND WITH ALL YOUR MIND" and to "LOVE YOUR NEIGHBOR AS YOURSELF" (Matthew 22:37, 39).

We can't stop with loving God; we must love each other too. We will not spend eternity in heaven with God alone; we will have each other as well.

Human relationships will not be minimized in heaven. Instead, we should expect to see them magnified and perfected, without any sinful or self-serving cliques, competition, comparisons, or conflicts.

Jesus promised such fellowship: "I say to you that many will come from east and west, and recline at the table with Abraham, Isaac and Jacob in the kingdom of heaven" (Matthew 8:11). How enjoyable will that be? Imagine that entertaining conversation!

In the coming kingdom, Abraham, Isaac, and Jacob will still be Abraham, Isaac, and Jacob. Notice they still have bodies that recline at tables—and there still are tables at which to recline. And evidently, there will be food on the tables, where we will eat, talk, laugh, enjoy each other, and make new friends. Imagine one day in heaven making new friends—and they happen to be Abraham, Isaac, and Jacob.

One author wrote: "We will experience all the best of human relationships, with none of the worst. . . . We'll be free of what displeases God and damages relationships."[1]

Paul preached that God orchestrates much more of our lives than we often consider: "And He made from one man every nation of mankind to live on all the face of the earth, having determined their appointed times and the boundaries of their habitation" (Acts 17:26).

God determined the time and exact place where you would live. It was no accident that you lived in that neighborhood, attended that school, sat next to those kids, had those teachers, and attended that church in which you made those friends in the youth group, the ladies Bible study, or the men's small group.

One of my sons is a church planter in Charlotte, North Carolina. One day he stepped into an elevator and saw a young man dressed for playing soccer. Ben struck up a conversation with him and discovered they had competed against each other in collegiate soccer leagues while in school. It was a divine appointment, and a new friendship was made.

It was no coincidence that he was not only in the right city and the right apartment complex but also in the right elevator at just the right time.

Beloved, your relationships were appointed by God. Those relationships among believers will continue in heaven—perfected and redeemed in every aspect.

Imagine all the *new* friendships to be discovered and enjoyed throughout eternity. And that implies you haven't even met some of your closest friends yet. Maybe you're disappointed because you've never had the friendships you longed for. God will answer that desire, not necessarily on this old earth, but certainly in the new earth and throughout eternity.[2] Maybe God has your assigned seat at the marriage supper of the Lamb next to someone you haven't yet met but who will become your closest friend for the next ten million years.[3]

And what about your family? You will, of course, remember your family. You won't need to be reintroduced to your believing family members, just as Abraham will not need to be reintroduced to his son Isaac and Jacob won't have to remind Isaac that Isaac is his father. You will remember your spouse, children, mother, father, siblings, and extended family. But those relationships will be healed where healing is needed, mended where mending is needed, and there will be forgiveness where forgiveness is needed.

Though you won't be obligated to your family in the same way or be married to your spouse, you will share in the memories of God's grace and rejoice in all that your believing parents, children, spouse, or family members have become!

Jonathan Edwards, the church leader and theologian of the eighteenth-century Great Awakening, wrote:

> There [will be] the Christian father, and mother, and wife, and child, and friend, with whom we shall renew the holy fellowship of the saints, which was interrupted by death here, but shall be commenced again in the upper sanctuary [heaven], and then shall never end.[4]

Relationships with believers will remain—and deepen—in heaven. God created us to enjoy fellowship, not only with Him but with others.

WILL BABIES WHO DIE GO TO HEAVEN?

While many believers have struggled with the question of whether infants who die go to heaven, the biblical answer is absolutely *yes*.

After experiencing the loss of his infant son, David announced in faith that he would go to him eventually: "I will go to him, but he will not return to me" (2 Samuel 12:23). David didn't say he would go to the grave but that he would go to *him*.

While the baby was extremely ill, David fasted, but David stopped fasting after his son died. Why? Because he knew that they would be reunited one day. So, he sorrowed, yet not as those who have no hope (1 Thessalonians 4:13).

Years later, Absalom, one of David's adult sons, died. In this instance, David grieved greatly, almost uncontrollably (2 Samuel 18:33–19:4). No doubt, one reason for this was that he knew he would never see this rebellious, evil son again. In contrast to this, David declared a coming reunion with his deceased infant son.

The grace of God, built upon the foundation and merits of Jesus Christ's atoning work, redeems not only those who *will* believe but also those who *cannot* believe. This includes individuals who are not old enough or not mentally capable of defying God and joining in the rebellion of unbelievers, who perceive the truth of the work of creation and yet deny the Creator, leaving them without excuse (Romans 1:20).

So, the vast multitude of worshippers in heaven will include untold millions of stillborn, aborted, and miscarried babies, and those who have died as infants and little children, along with mentally handicapped people, both young and old. This is one of the ways God will fulfill His promise that worshippers in heaven will be represented by people from *every* clan, people group, language, and nation (Revelation 5:9-10).

WILL I HAVE ANY MEMORIES OF MY LIFE ON EARTH?

Your first thought might be, *I hope I never remember my life on earth!* But there is a continuity between life now and the life to come. You are who you are because of all that God appointed for your life. You are the result of what you have done, enjoyed, suffered, failed, endured, and survived. Memory, therefore, is basic to your personality.[5]

Even in His glorified body, Jesus Christ didn't forget He was crucified. In fact, He kept some of His scars. They are not to remind *Him* of that awful death; they are eternal reminders to us of what He did on earth. Seeing His scars will remind us that our sin compelled Him to endure the cross, and we will love Him all the more.

We will not have to be reminded in heaven that we lost a baby or suffered through a painful illness. We will remember those events with even greater clarity than ever before, having perfected minds. But recalling earthly troubles and sorrows will not depress us in heaven. Instead, these things will deepen our joy as we come to understand God's wisdom through each difficulty, failure, and sorrow.

Many people have been confused on this matter by Isaiah 65:17, which reads: "For behold, I create new heavens and a new earth; and the former things will not be remembered or come to mind." This verse is often taken as indicating that none of us will remember anything (certainly not troubling things!) from our past lives on earth. The context of this verse, however, makes it clear that it is not referring to *us* but to God. In this context, *God* is choosing to forget our past sins. The previous verse clarifies the interpretation of verse 17: "Because the former troubles are forgotten, and because they are hidden from My sight!" (Isaiah 65:16).

God has chosen not to dwell on our sins or hold them against us.

The prophet Jeremiah quoted God saying something similar to what Isaiah recorded: "Their sin I will remember no more" (Jeremiah 31:34). God will never deal with us based on our sin but based on His Son's atoning death on our behalf.

What about the memories of our past?

One day we will stand before our Lord and give an account for our lives of service (Romans 14:12). This implies the act of remembering.

As believers we are encouraged by the truth that every good thing we do for Christ will be personalized and represented in our wedding garments (Revelation 19:8). Clearly, God wants us to remember those deeds forever—He's promised to weave them into our heavenly regalia. Perhaps those garments will include insignia, chords, and colors depicting some office, deed, sacrifice, ministry, or act of service performed for someone else. But clearly, God desires to reward us for everything we have done in His name (Hebrews 6:10).

The joy of heaven does not depend on an erased memory but on a renewed mind and a perfected perspective of what God was doing in our lives on earth.[6]

WILL THERE BE ANIMALS IN HEAVEN?

Absolutely! Heaven includes a new earth. The heavenly city will rest upon a newly formed earth (Revelation 21). The curse of sin has been reversed and God's new creation will mirror His original creation, with plenty of animals.

God will give the immortalized animal kingdom the ability to praise Him with elevated awareness and expression. The psalmist

David refers to all of creation rendering praise to God in their own unique voices of praise (Psalm 148).[7]

In the book of Revelation, John recorded a scene in which all the redeemed believers sing along with the angels. But they are not the only ones singing.

> Every created thing which is in heaven and on the earth and under the earth and on the sea, and all things in them, I heard saying, "To Him who sits on the throne, and to the Lamb, be blessing and honor and glory and dominion forever and ever." (Revelation 5:13)

This verse makes it clear: animals from all over the planet—in the skies, on the earth, under the earth, and on the sea, those crawling, running, galloping, flying, and swimming—will be in the new earth and heaven.

This is the garden of Eden . . . and so much more!

All of creation will sing praises to their creator God. All of creation will live the dream, a dream that was lost but has now been redeemed and re-created.

WILL MY PET BE IN HEAVEN?

My initial (tongue-in-cheek) answer to this question is, *it depends.* Some animals really will have to be converted; otherwise, they will ruin heaven for us all. I won't single out any animal specifically (least of all those purring felines that quietly rule the household).

A member of my home church sent me a funny story. I thought it summed up the whole question perfectly.

Three animals appeared before God's glorious golden throne of splendor—a German shepherd, a Doberman pinscher, and a cat. God said to the German shepherd, "What do *you* believe?" The German shepherd replied, "I believe in discipline and order." Then God asked the Doberman pin-scher, "What do *you* believe?" The Doberman answered, "I believe in protection and loyalty." Finally, God said to the cat, "What do *you* believe?" The cat said, "I believe you're in my seat." Yes, that pretty much sums up my thoughts on the matter!

Will some of our pets end up in the new heaven? We're not told.

Authors like John Piper, C. S. Lewis, John Wesley, and many church leaders before them have considered it a real possibility. They have argued that it would only be fitting for God to not only create entirely new animals in the new earth but also to bring back to life animals that suffered and groaned for the day of redemption (Romans 8:19-23).

The speculation goes along these lines: Why not allow some animals to enjoy the culmination of God's redemptive plan? The animals that once belonged to believers would be the perfect candidates to see and experience the reversal of the curse, which had so affected them as well. So might they not be among those animals John saw in heaven who sing praise to their creator God?

No doubt you've heard of Helen Keller, the blind and deaf girl who learned to communicate through the help of Anne Sullivan, who became her lifelong friend. Anne Sullivan took this restless, angry, frustrated child and patiently taught her by spelling words into the palm of her hand. Eventually, Helen came to understand the connection between the letters drawn on her hand and the objects around her.

When Anne finally taught Helen enough words to communicate, Anne asked a local pastor to come and deliver the gospel to this seven-year-old girl. As the truth of God's Word and the work of Jesus Christ was communicated to Helen through Anne's interpretation, the girl believed the gospel and was saved.

Helen told Anne this remarkable truth: she knew there was a God, but now she knew His name.

Later in life, Helen wrote:

> For three things I thank God every day of my life: thanks that he has vouchsafed me knowledge of his works; deep thanks that he has set in my darkness the lamp of faith; deep, deepest thanks that I have another life to look

forward to—a life joyous with light and flowers and heavenly song.[8]

At that moment when we step into the eternity of heaven, we, and all of nature together with us, will begin to live the dream—a dream that will *become* reality. We will live happily ever after, and happily ever after will last forever and ever.

CHAPTER TWELVE

LIFE IN THE FATHER'S HOUSE

Aproper study of our Creator and His amazing creation places God in the center and on the throne. The only other option is to place man in the center and on the throne. As evolutionist philosopher Ray Kurzweil said in a panel discussion, "The universe has been set up in an exquisitely specific way so that evolution could produce the people that are sitting here today and we could use our intelligence to talk about the universe."[1]

Consider the irony of that statement—*the universe has been set up in an exquisitely specific way* so that random mutations and millions of accidents over billions of years could produce intelligent people like us!

Kurzweil added with even more bravado that our intelligence is "a powerful force and we can see that its power is going to grow not linearly but exponentially, and will ultimately be powerful enough to change the destiny of the universe."[2]

In other words, we will keep evolving to such a high level of intelligence that eventually we will be smart enough to determine what happens to the universe.

According to the only eyewitness at the creation of the universe—God—our understanding of the future depends on an understanding of the past.

We can know the universe's future only when we start with what God says about its beginning: "In the beginning God created the heavens and the earth" (Genesis 1:1).

- *In the beginning God*—there is divine intelligence.
- *In the beginning God created*—there is divine power.
- *In the beginning God created the heavens and the earth*—there is divine planning.

According to Colossians, it was God the Son who spoke into empty space and said, "Let there be light," and it was so (Colossians 1:15-17).

This is the same Jesus who delivered this promise to His disciples:

> In My Father's house are many dwelling places; if it were not so, I would have told you; for I go to prepare a place for you. If I go and prepare a place for you, I will come again and receive you to Myself, that where I am, there you may be also. (John 14:2-3)

Later in his life, the apostle John was given a personal tour of this city of gold—the Father's house—which he describes in Revelation 21.

The new heaven is already finished; it is not evolving, and it is not under construction either. John writes, "Then I saw a new heaven and a new earth; for the first heaven and the first earth passed away" (Revelation 21:1).

John continues and describes in living color the sights and sounds of heaven—the Celestial City, the New Jerusalem adorned as a bride—which we also know as the Father's house.

Let's explore our future home and answer a few more questions about what life will be like in the Father's house.

A CITY OF BEAUTY

> And he carried me away in the Spirit to a great and high mountain, and showed me the holy city, Jerusalem, coming down out of heaven from God, having the glory of God. Her brilliance was like a very costly stone, as a stone of crystal-clear jasper. It had a great and high wall, with twelve gates, and at the gates twelve angels; and names were written on them, which are the names of the twelve tribes of the sons of Israel. (Revelation 21:10-12)

Though John does not tell how high this outer wall is, he does tell us it is "seventy-two yards" thick (verse 17). Literally, this reads 144 cubits, which means it could be anywhere from 216 to 250 feet thick.

The wall has twelve gates hinged to it, three on each of the four sides of the city (verse 13). Each gate is made of a single pearl matching the thickness of the wall.

We're not even inside the house yet and are staggered by the gates. Each gate is crafted out of a single pearl with a diameter of well over two hundred feet![3]

What kind of oyster could make a pearl of such magnitude? The truth is, an oyster could never make a pearl like this—even in a million years. But Jesus does—in a moment. Even though He creates a real pearl, He does so by transcending the normal processes of time and matter, just as He did when He created real bread and real fish in his hands, thousands of times, in order to feed more than five thousand people. That bread was as real as if it had been baked in the oven; that fish was as real as if it had been freshly caught from the sea and pickled, as they did in the first century, to eat with their barley bread.

But why would the Lord use pearls for doors into the celestial city?

Of all the precious gems John mentions in Revelation, the pearl is the only that is normally formed by a *living* creature. When a tiny grain of sand enters its shell, the oyster layers over and around that uncomfortable intruder again and again with calcium carbonate. The result is a pearl.[4]

The pearl is something beautiful created out of something *painful*; it's the oyster's answer to whatever injured it.[5] Similarly, heaven is the answer of God to that which injured our crucified Lord. Jesus bore the greatest possible irritations of sin and wrath for our sake. Something beautiful came out of something painful.

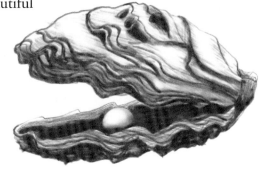

Beauty out of tribulation

Each time we enter the Father's house through one of those twelve pearly gates, we will be reminded that Jesus Christ was born on earth to suffer and die so that a doorway into heaven could be opened by faith.

A CITY OF IMPRESSIVE STRUCTURE

But John revealed more than the gates; he also recorded the measurements of the holy city:

An artist's depiction of New Jerusalem

The city is laid out as a square, and its length is as great as the width; and he measured the city with the rod, fifteen hundred miles; its length and width and height are equal. (Revelation 21:16)

I believe the fifteen hundred miles here are the total cubic miles of the city; that is, the sum of the length, width, and height of the city multiplied together.[6] This would mean both the length and depth of the Father's house extend about eleven miles and the top of the house stretches about eleven miles high, reaching upward through our current atmosphere.

The tallest skyscraper mankind has built thus far is the Burj Khalifa tower in Dubai. It stands 2,717 feet high and has 163 floors. The tallest mountain in the world, Mount Everest, stuns anyone with its massive structure and height. It would take ten towers of Dubai stacked on top of each other to reach the height of Mount Everest—just over 29,000 feet.

The Celestial City—the Father's house—will be far more impressive than Mount Everest. You would have to stack one Mount Everest on top of another before you would reach the apex of the Father's house. With a height of over eleven miles, it would appear there are twelve levels, or "floors," in the city, each with its own foundation (verse 14). You would be able to put hundreds of Burj Khalifas into the first floor of the twelve levels of the Father's house and still have plenty of room to spare.

The apostle John added that the river of life will flow from the Father's throne. Can you imagine the water cascading down each level with waterfalls a mile high?

On each side of that river flowing through the center of the Celestial City, orchards of trees will bear fruit every single month, representing the tree of life.

In John 14, the Lord promised His disciples they would have a dwelling place in the Father's house. Many Bible versions render the Greek word *monē* (meaning "dwelling place" or "room") as "mansion."

This promise of the Lord that we will live in His Father's house is rooted in the imagery of the first-century Jewish wedding. During the *kiddushim*, which was the betrothal or engagement period, the young man built a dwelling place onto his father's house. When it was time to celebrate his marriage, he collected his bride and, after the ceremony and feasting, brought her back to live *in* the family home.

The city of God John the apostle describes will settle in Jerusalem on a newly created and raised plateau after the Lord changes the topography of the region (see Zechariah 14:10). Even though this city has not appeared yet, it will descend and hover over Jerusalem during the millennial kingdom. After the earth and the universe are destroyed and recreated, it will settle on a New Jerusalem, where we will have a dwelling place forever.

We are not informed about the size of our personal dwelling places in the Father's house. What we do know is that every believer will have a home address in the Father's house. In the meantime, believers who die go immediately to be with their Lord in heaven. As Paul indicated, to be absent from the body means to be present with the Lord (2 Corinthians 5:8). They are already enjoying the Celestial City.

A CITY OF REMEMBRANCE

> And the wall of the city had twelve foundation stones,
> and on them were the twelve names of the twelve apos-
> tles of the Lamb. (Revelation 21:14)

It's fascinating that the gates and the foundation stones have no
Scripture verses engraved on them. Instead, the only engraving in the
structure of the Father's house are names—names of people.

God intends us to remember the names of the twelve sons (tribes)
of Israel (verse 12) and the twelve apostles (verse 14). Every time we
go up to the floor where the foundation stone has engraved on it the
name *Peter*, we will remember Peter and, no doubt, his sin. However,
our memories will be perfected in holiness, so we will not dwell on
his sin but on the faithful forgiveness and grace of Christ in Peter's
life—and ours.

The glory of God will be reflected in the memories, histories,
and redemption of sinners. All the redeemed of the Old and New
Testament eras will be represented in the architecture of the Father's
house.

Some believe we will remember only positive things. But consider
the Mount of Transfiguration.

Peter, James, and John accompanied the Lord Jesus up the mountain, where Jesus was joined by Moses and Elijah. Moses had died
some 1450 years prior to this, and Elijah had been taken to heaven
more than 800 years before this moment. On this occasion, they met
with Jesus, robed in glorious splendor, and the clothing and visage of
the transfigured Lord were as bright as lightning (Matthew 17).

What did they talk about?

According to Luke's Gospel, they talked about Jesus' coming
departure from Jerusalem, a reference to His crucifixion, resurrection,
and ascension (Luke 9:31).

They were still Moses and Elijah; they did not need an introduction to Jesus. And they knew what was going to happen next, along
with all the suffering and sorrow involved. They knew what Jesus was
about to face in the events of Christ's suffering and death.

In Revelation 18, an angel points to the events happening on earth during the tribulation period, and tells the believers in heaven to rejoice over the judgment of God upon the earth (verse 20). Evidently, they can observe to some degree these significant (and terrible) events.

In the following chapter, which tells of God's judgment upon the empire of Satan and the Antichrist during the tribulation, we read about the roar of a great multitude in heaven, saying, "Hallelujah! Salvation and glory and power belong to our God; BECAUSE HIS JUDGMENTS ARE TRUE AND RIGHTEOUS" (Revelation 19:1-2). People in heaven are evidently very aware of the wrath of God and the judgment of the defiant human race on earth.

Again, *during* the tribulation, millions of people will come to faith in Christ and then be martyred for it. The apostle John hears the powerful prayer of these martyred saints around the throne of God:

> "How long, O Lord, holy and true, will You refrain from
> judging and avenging our blood on those who dwell on
> the earth?" (Revelation 6:10)

These individuals are in heaven, but their words and actions make it clear they know what's happening on earth. And here we see them praying for God's holy justice to be displayed and their deaths avenged.

- They know that judgment has not been completed on earth.
- They pray for the Lord to act in justice.
- They are praying, as it were, and having to wait for an answer.
- They are aware of the violence on earth and the reign of evil taking place.

None of this *ruins* heaven for them. Future happiness in heaven is not based on our failure to know what is happening on earth but on seeing the earth with new eyes and with the righteous perspective of our Lord.

With perfected hearts and glorified minds, we will see everything in light of who God is, and we will glory in the grace of God for the redeemed and look to the justice of God toward the unredeemed with equal admiration.

The Celestial City will be a place of remembrance!

Our happiness in heaven will not depend on a memory swipe so that we never remember anything about our lives on earth. Our memories make us who we are. We will be reminded and then rewarded for everything we did on earth that was in obedience to Christ. Our happiness in heaven will be based on Christ's forgiveness, and our perception of His forgiveness will be perfected and deepened, liberating and freeing, for we shall see Him, embrace Him, worship Him, and be secure in Him forever.

The joy of heaven is not based on our *ignorance* but on new *understanding*.[7] The grace and glory of Christ will only be that much more brilliant, beautiful, and amazing.

Just as Jesus Christ remembered and loved His disciples after He was resurrected and glorified, so we will remember our lives together as believers, family members, church members, and fellow laborers.

Our minds and hearts will be forever cleansed, glorified, and perfected, never to be stained again with the slightest sin; we will continually develop, learn, and experience a deeper awareness of God's forgiveness and the ability to forgive one another. We will rejoice in our experiences of the past and in the glorious splendor of the Father's house.

Unlike the first creation, this new creation will not have the potential of another Lucifer rebelling or another Adam and Eve sinning.[8]

Never again. The gospel is completed. Salvation is once and for all. Our perfection and eternal glorification are guaranteed, and forever we will enjoy heaven on a new earth surrounded by a new universe.

And the centerpiece of it all—our creator God—will be our source of joy. Around His throne we will worship without inhibition. Our lives will finally be unfettered by iniquity, our hearts will be free without impurity, and our service for Him will be without inconsistency.

And our forever home, the new earth and the new universe, will be ours to explore, revel in, and enjoy without end . . . In Living Color!

ENDNOTES

INTRODUCTION

1 "Leonardo Da Vinci, His Life and Artworks," www.leonardodavinci.net/.

2 *The Notebooks of Leonardo Da Vinci*, Volume 1, translated by Jean Paul Richter (1888), digital format produced by Charles Aldarondo and the Distributed Proofreaders team, 1021–24.

3 Mark Batterson, Richard Foth, and Susanna Foth Aughtmon, *A Trip Around the Sun* (Baker, 2015), 143.

4 James Montgomery Boice, *Psalms Volume 1: Psalms 1–41* (Baker, 1994), 161.

5 Phillip Keller, *Still Waters* (Revell, 1980), 133.

6 Willem A. VanGemeren, "Psalms," in *The Expositor's Bible Commentary*, ed. Frank E. Gaebelein, volume 5 (Zondervan, 1991), 180.

7 Monica Grady, "What Does the Solar System Sound Like?" The Conversation, July 27, 2016, https://theconversation.com.

8 Ethan Siegel, "There Is Sound in Space, Thanks to Gravitational Waves," *Forbes*, May 2, 2017, www.forbes.com.

9 "Spooky Space Sounds," NASA, October 26, 2017, www.nasa.gov..

10 Allen P. Ross, *A Commentary on The Psalms: Volume 3* (Kregel, 2016), 366.

11 Charles Spurgeon, *The Treasury of David,* Volume 3 (Zondervan, 1977), 2.

12 Quoted in Javier Ordovas, "25 Famous Scientists on God," *Aleteia*, June 26, 2016.

13 Carl Sagan, *Pale Blue Dot: A Vision of the Human Future in Space* (Random House, 1994), 7.

14 Mark Batterson, *The Grave Robber* (Baker Books, 2014), 19.

15 Maltbie D. Babcock, "This Is My Father's World."

16 Cited in Avery Foley, "Wired for Awe," Answers in Genesis, March 1, 2018, https://answersingenesis.org.

17 Ibid.

18 Isaac Watts, "I Sing the Mighty Power of God."

CHAPTER ONE

1 Donald B. DeYoung, *Thousands . . . Not Billions* (Master Books, 2005), 13.

2 "Uniformitarianism: Charles Lyell," Understanding Evolution, evolution.berkeley.edu.

3 Wayne Ranney, "How Old Is the Grand Canyon?" Geology.com.

4 The above observations and thoughts are adapted from John D. Morris, *The Geology Book* (Master Books, 2007), 25-65.

[5] The editors of *Encyclopaedia Britannica*, "Catastrophism," brittanica.com.

[6] Andrew Turgeon and Elizabeth Morse, "Coal, National Geographic, nationalgeographic.org.

[7] Quotes in the "Introduction" to Rob Carson, *Mount St. Helens: The Eruption and Recovery of a Volcano* (Sasquatch Books, 2015).

[8] Andrew A. Snelling, "Vertical Floaters," in "Lasting Lessons from Mount St. Helens," by Andrew Snelling, Joe Francis, and Tom Hennigan, Answers in Genesis, April 1, 2015, answersingenesis.org.

[9] Ibid.

[10] Andrew A. Snelling, "Bark Peat," in "Lasting Lessons from Mount St. Helens," by Andrew Snelling, Joe Francis, and Tom Hennigan, Answers in Genesis, April 1, 2015, answersingenesis.org.

[11] Ibid.

[12] Andrew A. Snelling, "New Lava Dome with Old Radiometric Dates," in "Lasting Lessons from Mount St. Helens," by Andrew Snelling, Joe Francis, and Tom Hennigan, Answers in Genesis, April 1, 2015, answersingenesis.org. See also John Morris, *The Geology Book*, 52.

[13] Ibid.

[14] Simon Worrall, "Mistakes Led to Needless Deaths from Worst Volcanic Blast," *National Geographic*, May 20, 2016, nationalgeographic.com; Ed Leckert, "The Mountain Ain't Gonna Hurt Me," Ed Leckert Images, August 26, 2014, edleckertimages.com.

CHAPTER TWO

[1] Ken Ham, "Earth: Just Right for Life," Answers in Genesis, April 3, 2016, answersingenesis.org.

[2] Danny Faulkner, "A Unique Blend," Answers in Genesis, January 1, 2014, answersingenesis.org.

[3] Ibid.

[4] Ibid.

[5] Danny Faulkner, "A Perfect Partner," Answers in Genesis, January 1, 2014, answersingenesis.org.

[6] John H. Tiner, *Isaac Newton: Inventor, Scientist, and Teacher* (Mott Media, 1975), 107.

[7] John MacArthur Jr., *The Battle for the Beginning: The Bible on Creation and the Fall of Man* (Thomas Nelson, 2005), 112.

[8] Jerry Bergman, "The Moon: Required for Life on Earth," *Acts & Facts* 47 (10), October 2018, 10-13.

[9] Quoted in Lesley Alderman, *The Book of Times: From Seconds to Centuries, A Compendium of Measures* (William Morrow, 2013), 311.

[10] "What Is Jupiter?" NASA, August 10, 2011, nasa.gov.

[11] Ibid.

[12] "Jupiter's Great Red Spot: A Swirling Mystery," NASA, August 4, 2015, nasa.gov.

[13] MacArthur, 111.

[14] "Pistol Star," Constellation Guide, August 4, 2017, constellation-guide.com; "Pistol Star," solstation.com.

[15] Elizabeth Howell, "Antares: Red Star at the End of Its Life," Space.com, August 18, 2017, space.com.

[16] "Joining Forces for Science: Jill Tarter and Margaret Turnbull," SETI Institute, September 24, 2018, seti.org.

[17] See Jason Lisle, *Taking Back Astronomy* (Master Books, 2006), 91-98.

[18] Seth Shostak, "Fermi Paradox," SETI Institute, April 19, 2018, seti.org.

[19] David Klinghoffer, "Alien Octopodes and the Multiverse," Evolution News and Science Today, July 9, 2018, evolutionnews.org.

[20] Louis Giglio, "Indescribable," sermon transcript.

CHAPTER THREE

[1] Ken Ham, *Dinosaurs* (Answers in Genesis, 2010), 13.

[2] Ken Ham, *Dinosaurs for Kids* (Answers in Genesis, 2009), 31.

[3] Ibid, 68.

[4] Quoted in Ken Ham, *Dinosaurs of Eden* (Master Books, 2001), 35.

[5] Ibid, 31.

[6] M. H. Schweitzer, et al., "Biomolecular Characterization and Protein Sequences of the Campanian Hadrosaur B," *Science* 234:626–31.

[7] Henry M. Morris, quoted in Ken Ham, *Dinosaurs*, 80.

[8] John MacArthur, *The Battle for the Beginning: The Bible on Creation and the Fall of Adam* (Thomas Nelson, 2005), 151.

[9] Natan Slifkin, *Sacred Monsters: Mysterious and Mythical Creatures of Scripture, Talmud and Midrash* (Torah/Gefen Books, 2011) 198.

[10] David Atkinson, *The Message of Job* (InterVarsity Press, 1991), 147.

[11] Max Lucado, *The Great House of God: A Home for Your Heart* (Thomas Nelson, 1997), 40.

CHAPTER FOUR

[1] Kevin Dennehy, "F&ES Study Reveals There Are Many More Trees Than Previously Believed," Yale School of Forestry and Environmental Studies," environment.yale.edu.

2 "Should Christians 'Love a Tree'?" Answers in Genesis, May 15, 2019, answersingenesis.org.

3 Quoted in Marlene Cimons, "Tracing the Evolution of Forest Trees," National Science Foundation, November 7, 2014, nsf.gov.

4 Frank Sherwin, "Trees: An Engineering Wonder," *Acts & Facts* 44 (9), September 2015, 9-10.

5 "Sensational Australian Tree . . . 'Like Finding a Live Dinosaur,'" Answers in Genesis, May 1, 1995, answersingenesis.org.

6 Tom Hennigan, "Talking Trees—Secrets of Plant Communication," Answers in Genesis, April 9, 2017, answersingenesis.org.

7 Ibid.

8 Ibid.

9 Ibid.

CHAPTER FIVE

1 "Aeolus in Greek Mythology," Greek Legends and Myths, greeklegendsandmyths.com.

2 "ADM-Aeolus," Wikipedia, en.wikipedia.org.

3 "What Is the Origin of the Phrase 'It's Raining Cats and Dogs'?" Library of Congress, Everyday Mysteries, loc.gov.

4 Erwin Lutzer, *Where Was God? Answers to Tough Questions about God and Natural Disasters* (Tyndale House, 2006), xiii.

5 Lutzer, 21.

6 The source of this familiar quote is unknown, though it is often attributed to Charles Spurgeon.

7 Chris Clayton, "Who Is Sonny Perdue?" Northern Ag Network, January 22, 2017, northernag.net.

8 Rick Perry, "A Message from Governor Rick Perry," in Donna Calvin, "A Special Call to Fast and Pray," beliefnet.com.

9 John Fletcher, "Voltaire, L'esprit, and Irony," Oxford University Press Blog, November 21, 2012, blog.oup.com.

10 Henry M. Morris, *The Genesis Record* (Baker, 1976), 127.

11 Augustus M. Toplady, "Rock of Ages."

CHAPTER SIX

1 Jonathan Edwards, *Basic Writings*, selected and edited by Ola Winslow (New American Library, 1966), 33.

2 Ibid., 85.

[3] "Honey Trivia," British Honey Importing and Packers Association, honeyassociation.com.

[4] Holley Bishop, *Robbing the Bees: A Biography of Honey—The Sweet Liquid Gold that Seduced the World* (Free Press, 2005), 193.

[5] Tom Hennigan, "A Sweet Revelation," *Creation Magazine* 21:4 (September 1999), 48.

[6] Ibid.

[7] Bruce Waltke, *The Book of Proverbs* (Eerdmans, 2004), 337.

[8] John Ortberg, "Intercepting Entropy," Sermon Illustrations, preachingtoday.com.

[9] This process is described by Tom Hennigan, "Ants—Millimeter Messengers," Answers in Genesis, September 2, 2014, answersingenesis.org.

[10] Ortberg.

CHAPTER SEVEN

[1] Timothy R. Jennings, *The God Shaped Heart* (Baker Books, 2017), 24.

[2] Gerhard Kittel, ed., *Theological Dictionary of the New Testament*, Volume 4 (Eerdmans, 1967), 755.

[3] Charles R. Swindoll, *New Testament Insights: Romans* (Zondervan, 2010), 113.

[4] Adapted from Gordon Wilson, "Metamorphosis—A Symphony of Miracles," Answers in Genesis, April 1, 2014 answersingenesis.org; Ferris Jabr, "How Does a Caterpillar Turn into a Butterfly?" *Scientific American*, August 10, 2012, scientificamerican.com; "Butterfly Life Cycle/Butterfly Metamorphosis," The Butterfly Site, thebutterflysite.com.

[5] Neil Postman, "Science and the Story that We Need," *First Things* (January 1997), firstthings.com.

[6] David Kinnaman and Gabe Lyons, *Good Faith* (Baker Books, 2016), 58.

CHAPTER EIGHT

[1] Quoted in John Stott, *The Birds Our Teachers* (Hendrickson Publishers, 2007), 37.

[2] Fritz Rienecker and Cleon Rogers, *Linguistic Key to the Greek New Testament* (Regency, 1976), 19.

[3] Quoted in Stott, 10.

[4] Ibid.

[5] Quoted in Charles R. Swindoll, *Tale of the Tardy Oxcart* (Word Publishing, 1998), 319.

[6] Stott, 48.

[7] Crawford H. Greenewalt, *Hummingbirds* (Dover Publications, 1990), 9.

[8] Stott, 70.

[9] Pliny the Elder, *Natural History*, Perseus Digital Library, perseus.tufts.edu.

[10] Stott, 68.

[11] Quoted in Stott, 68.

[12] Henry Chichester Hart, *The Animals Mentioned in the Bible* (Aeterna Press, 2015), 89.

[13] Stott, 18.

[14] Ibid., 22.

CHAPTER NINE

[1] Augustine, *Confessions*, ed. Michael P. Foley, second edition (Hackett Publishing Company, Inc.), 2006, 10.8.15.

[2] Tommy Mitchell, "Didn't Darwin Call the Evolution of the Eye Absurd?" Answers in Genesis, September 14, 2010, answersingenesis.org.

[3] Ibid.

[4] Bertrand Russel, *Religion and Science* (Oxford University Press, 1961), 222.

[5] Quoted in Russel Stannard, *Science and Wonders* (Faber and Faber, 1996), 7.

[6] Michael Denton, *Evolution: A Theory in Crisis* (Adler and Adler, 1986), 328-29.

[7] Genomics Primer, "DNA Definition," helio.com; Encyclopedia Britannica, "DNA Chemical Compound," Britannica.com.

[8] DNA Worldwide, "The History of DNA Timeline," dna-worldwide.com; What Is Epigenetics? "A Super Brief and Basic Explanation of Epigenetics for Total Beginners," whatisepigenetics.com.

[9] "A Super Brief and Basic Explanation of Epigenetics for Total Beginners."

[10] Hannah Ashworth, "How Long is Your DNA?" Science Focus, sciencefocus.com.

[11] Michael Guillen, "Did A Mysterious Extinction Event Precede Adam and Eve?" Fox News, November 24, 2018, foxnews.com.

CHAPTER TEN

[1] Randy Alcorn, *Heaven* (Tyndale House, 2004), 281.

[2] See John MacArthur, *The Glory of Heaven* (Crossway, 1996), 130.

[3] Alcorn, 45.

[4] MacArthur, 133.

[5] Alcorn, 286.

[6] Ibid.

[7] Ibid., 430.

[8] Ray Stedman, "The City of Glory," raystedman.org.

CHAPTER ELEVEN

[1] Randy Alcorn, *Heaven* (Tyndale, 2004), 353.

[2] Ibid., 343.

[3] Ibid.

[4] Quoted in ibid., 329.

[5] Ibid., 331.

[6] Ibid., 332.

[7] Ron Rhodes, *The Little Book About Heaven* (Harvest House, 2013), 41.

[8] Quoted in Alcorn, *Heaven*, 417.

CHAPTER TWELVE

[1] Ray Kurzweil, "The Intelligent Universe," Edge.org, November 5, 2002.

[2] Ibid.

[3] Grant R. Osborne, *Revelation*, Baker Exegetical Commentary on the New Testament (Baker, 2002), 758.

[4] John Phillips, *Exploring Revelation* (Kregel, 1987), 254.

[5] Adapted from Ray C. Stedman, *God's Final Word: Understanding Revelation* (Discovery House, 1991), 344.

[6] See Janet Willis, *What on Earth Is Heaven Like?* (Khesed Publications, 2013). 44-45. The NASB uses the round number "fifteen hundred miles" to render the Greek text's "twelve thousand stadia," which is probably somewhat less than fifteen hundred miles.

[7] Ibid.

[8] Nathan M. Meyer, *From Now to Eternity* (BMH Books, 1976), 203.